IN MEMORY OF:

   Ransom and Ann Oetzel

PRESENTED BY:

Mr. and Mrs. Terry Oetzel
and
Family

Women's
Firsts

10/00

Women's Firsts

Firsts

MILESTONES
IN WOMEN'S
HISTORY

VOLUME 2

Media
Professions
Religion
Science
Sports

Peggy Saari, Tim & Susan Gall, Editors

U·X·L®

AN IMPRINT OF GALE

DETROIT · NEW YORK · TORONTO · LONDON

Women's Firsts: Milestones in Women's History

Peggy Saari, Tim L. Gall, and Susan B. Gall, Editors

Staff

Elizabeth Des Chenes, *U•X•L Developmental Editor*
Carol DeKane Nagel, *U•X•L Managing Editor*
Thomas L. Romig, *U•X•L Publisher*

Margaret Chamberlain, *Permissions Specialist*
Shalice Shah, *Permission Associate*

Shanna P. Heilveil, *Production Assistant*
Evi Seoud, *Assistant Production Manager*
Mary Beth Trimper, *Production Director*

Pamela A. E. Galbreath, *Senior Art Director*
Cynthia Baldwin, *Product Design Manager*

Linda Mahoney, *Typesetting*

Library of Congress Cataloging-in-Publication Data

Women's firsts: milestones in women's history/
Peggy Saari and Tim and Susan B. Gall , editors

p.   cm.
Includes bibliographical references and index.

Contents: v. 1. Activism-government v. 2. media-sports

ISBN 0-7876-0653-7 (set: alk paper).
ISBN 0-7876-0654-5 (vol. 1: alk paper)

ISBN 0-7876-0655-3 (vol. 2: alk paper)

1. Women—History—Miscellanea—Juvenile literature. 2. Women—History—Chronology— Juvenile Literature. 3. Women—Biography—Miscellanea—Juvenile Literature.

[1. Women—History.]

I. Saari, Peggy. II. Gall, Timothy L. III. Gall, Susan B.

HQ1121.W8858 1997
305.4'09—dc21

97-25479

CIP AC

⊗™ This book is printed on acid-free paper that meets the minimum requirements of American National Standard for Information Sciences–Permanence Paper for Printed Library Materials, ANSI Z39.48-1984.

Printed in the United States of America
10 9 8 7 6 5 4 3 2

Contents

Bold type indicates volume number

Bette Davis (see "The Arts: Film" entry dated 1941)

Volume 2

Reader's Guide

Anne Hutchinson (see "Religion: Founders and Leaders" entry dated 1635)

Women's Firsts: Milestones in Women's History provides information on over 1,000 milestones involving women around the world, from early history to the present. Both *Women's Firsts* volumes are divided into five chapters. Each of the ten chapters focuses on a specific theme: Activism, The Arts, Business, Education, Government, Media, Professions, Religion, Science and Technology, and Sports. Every chapter is divided into subject categories and entries summarize milestones and provide bibliographic information. Sidebar boxes examine related events and issues, while more than 140 black-and-white illustrations help enliven and explain the text. Both volumes contain a timeline of important events, a "words to know" section, and a cumulative index.

A Note about Researching Firsts

In compiling *Women's Firsts,* the editors tried to deal with sources critically and honestly to present the most representative and accurate list of firsts by women possible. Some probable firsts could not be included due to a lack of definitive proof. Beyond general error, differences among sources often occurred when there was uncertainty about which date to use or the criteria for claiming a first. Each entry in *Women's Firsts* was researched through multiple sources for accuracy, with the final content reflecting a majority point of view.

Acknowledgments

Special thanks are due for the invaluable comments and suggestions provided by U•X•L's women's books advisors:

Annette Haley, High School Librarian/Media Specialist at Grosse Ile High School in Grosse Ile, Michigan; Mary Ruthsdotter, Projects Director of the National Women's History Project; Francine Stampnitzky, Children's/Young Adult Librarian at the Elmont Public Library in Elmont, New York; and Ruth Ann Karlin Yeske, Librarian at North Middle School in Rapid City, South Dakota.

Additional thanks go to Stephen Allison for his extensive contributions to the book, and to Jon Saari for his continued writing and editing assistance.

Comments and Suggestions

We welcome your comments and suggestions for future editions of *Women's Firsts*. Please write: Editor, *Women's Firsts,* U•X•L, 835 Penobscot Bldg., Detroit, Michigan, 48226-4094; call toll free: 800-877-4253; or fax to: 313-961-6347.

Photo Credits

The photographs appearing in *Women's Firsts: Milestones in Women's History* were received from the following sources:

On the cover: Pearl S. Buck (**Courtesy of AP/Wide World Photos. Reproduced by permission.**); Lynette Woodard (**Courtesy of Corbis-Bettmann. Reproduced by permission.**); Juliette Gordon Low (**Courtesy of Girl Scouts, USA. Reproduced by permission.**)

AP/Wide World Photos. Reproduced by permission.: pp. v, ix, xiii, xiv, 26, 40, 42, 43, 52, 58, 60, 61, 64, 66, 68, 69, 71, 90, 98, 113, 114, 122, 171, 188, 191; 197; 201, 208, 211, 269, 272, 275, 309, 312, 313, 320, 321, 328, 334, 337, 339, 340, 341, 343, 361, 371, 408, 413; **Corbis-Bettmann. Reproduced by permission.:** pp. xi, xv, xvii, 82, 89, 110, 116, 120, 126, 237, 255, 291, 300, 356, 374, 383, 395, 409; **EPD Photos. Reproduced by permission.:** pp. 1, 45, 105, 109, 155, 159, 252, 256, 278, 373; **The Library of Congress. Reproduced by permission.:** pp. 2, 44, 50, 115, 241, 331, 332; **Camp Fire, Inc. Reproduced by permis-**

Clara Barton (see "Professions: Medicine and Health Care" entry dated 1881)

Women's Firsts: A Timeline of Events

c. 1351 B.C. Hebrew prophetess Deborah was the only female judge in ancient Israel.

Seventh century B.C. Greek physician Hygeia was the first person to teach preventive medicine.

First century A.D. Alexandrine alchemist Maria the Jewess was one of the founders of chemistry.

Early eleventh century Japanese noblewoman Shikibu Murasaki was the first novelist.

1559 Italian artist Sofonisba Anguissola was the first woman to become a famous professional painter.

Golda Meir (see "Government: Prime Ministers" entry dated 1969)

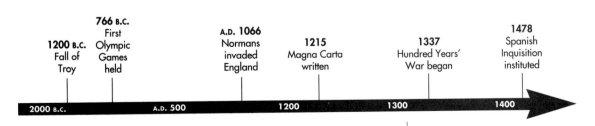

| 1200 B.C. Fall of Troy | 766 B.C. First Olympic Games held | A.D. 1066 Normans invaded England | 1215 Magna Carta written | 1337 Hundred Years' War began | 1478 Spanish Inquisition instituted |

2000 B.C. A.D. 500 1200 1300 1400

Marie Curie (see "Science and Technology: Physical Science" entry dated 1903)

1633 French aristocrat Louise de Marillac founded the Daughters of Charity.

c. 1675 Queen Anne (Totopotomoi) was the first woman to become a Native American chief.

1824 American activists Lavinia White and Louise Mitchell founded the first women's labor union.

1848 American feminists Lucretia Coffin Mott and Elizabeth Cady Stanton organized the first women's rights convention in the United States.

1854 British health care worker Florence Nightingale established modern nursing practices.

1879 American religious leader Mary Baker Eddy founded the Church of Christ, Scientist (also called Christian Science).

1882 Dutch physician Aletta Jacobs opened the world's first birth control clinic.

1896 French cinematographer Alice Guy-Blanché was the world's first female producer-director of motion pictures.

1908 American Annie Smith Peck climbed the north peak of Mount Huascaran in Peru.

1912 Italian educator Maria Montessori introduced her revolutionary teaching method.

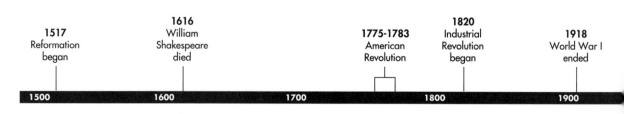

1517 Reformation began

1616 William Shakespeare died

1775-1783 American Revolution

1820 Industrial Revolution began

1918 World War I ended

1500 1600 1700 1800 1900

1916 Canadian lawyer Emily Gowan Murphy became the first female magistrate in the British Empire.

1920 Chinese political activist Jingyu Xiang cofounded the Chinese Communist Party.

1938 Austrian physicist Lise Meitner codeveloped the theory of nuclear fission.

1945 American mathematician Grace Brewster Murray Hopper developed operating programs for the first digital computer.

1951 English molecular biologist Rosalind Franklin helped determine the structure of DNA.

1959 American toymaker Ruth Handler created the Barbie Doll.

1963 Austrian conservationist Joy Adamson founded the World Wildlife Fund.

1966 Indian politician Indira Gandhi was elected the first woman leader of the world's largest democracy.

1970 Danish shoe designer Anna Kalso introduced the Earth Shoe.

1971 American journalist Gloria Steinem cofounded *Ms.* magazine.

1975 Australian pediatrician Helen Caldicott began her campaign against nuclear power and weapons.

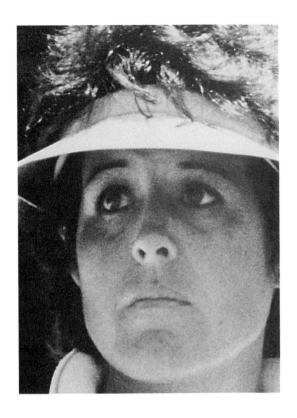

Nancy Lopez (see "Sports: Individual Sports" entry dated 1978)

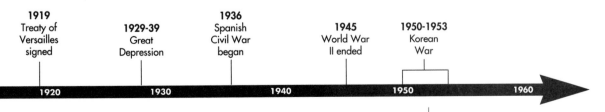

1919
Treaty of
Versailles
signed

1929-39
Great
Depression

1936
Spanish
Civil War
began

1945
World War
II ended

1950-1953
Korean
War

1920   1930   1940   1950   1960

1979 English politician Margaret Thatcher became the first female prime minister of Great Britain.

1981 American lawyer Sandra Day O'Connor was appointed the first woman Justice of the U.S. Supreme Court.

1982 Russian cosmonaut Svetlanta Saviskaya was the first woman to walk in space.

1983 American composer Ellen Taaffe Zwilich was the first woman to win a Pulitzer Prize for music.

1986 American chemist Susan Solomon identified the cause of the "hole" in the ozone layer.

1988 Pakistani political activist Benazir Bhutto became the first modern-day female leader of a Muslim nation.

1993 American executive Lucy Salhany became the first woman to head a national television network.

1996 American astronaut Shannon Lucid set a record for spending the longest time in space.

1997 American diplomat Madeleine Albright was appointed the first female U.S. Secretary of State.

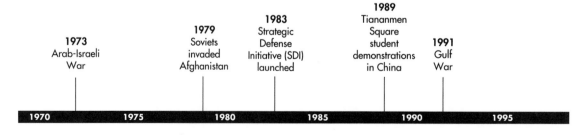

Words to Know

Christine Choy (see "The Arts: Film" entry dated c. 1970s)

A

Abolitionist: A person who supports putting an end to slavery.

Aeronautical engineer: An engineer who designs aircraft.

Anatomist: A scientist who studies the structure of organisms, including the human body.

Anthropologist: A scientist who studies human beings in relation to physical, environmental, social, and cultural characteristics.

Archaeologist: A scientist who studies the fossils, relics, and buildings of past civilizations.

Astronomer: A scientist who makes observations of objects and matter outside the earth's atmosphere.

B

Bacteriologist: A scientist who studies bacteria and their relationship to medicine, industry, and agriculture.

Biochemist: A scientist who studies chemical compounds and processes in living organisms.

Biologist: A scientist who studies plant and animal life.

Biophysicist: A scientist who applies physics to biological problems.

C

Choreographer: A person who creates dance movements and designs dance productions.

Christianity: The religion derived from the teachings of Jesus Christ, based on the Bible as sacred scripture, and professed by Eastern, Roman Catholic, and Protestant followers.

Cinematographer: The principle photographer on a telefilm or motion picture.

Convent: A community or house of nuns belonging to a religious order or congregation.

E

Epidemiologist: A medical scientist who studies the number and distribution of cases of disease within a population.

Exile: Forced absence from one's country or home.

F

Feminist: A person who supports the political, economic, and social equality of the sexes.

G

Geneticist: A biologist who studies the genetic makeup of an organism.

Geophysicist: A scientist who studies the physical properties of the earth and its environment.

H

Hinduism: The dominant religion of India that emphasizes mystical reflection and self discipline as a way to reach inner peace.

I

Islam: The religious faith of Muslims based on the belief in Allah as the sole deity and in Muhammad as his prophet.

J

Judaism: A religion developed among the ancient Hebrews and based on the belief in one God who revealed himself to Abraham, Moses, and the Hebrew prophets. Judaism encourages leading a religious life in accordance with the Scriptures and rabbinical traditions.

M

Marine biologist: A scientist who studies living organisms in the oceans and seas.

Medieval: Pertaining to the Middle Ages, the period of European history from about A.D. 500 to about 1500.

Meteorologist: A scientist who studies the atmosphere and makes weather predictions.

Mysticism: The belief that direct knowledge of God, spiritual truth, or ultimate reality can be attained through personal experience.

N

Naturalist: A scientist who studies nature and the environment.

Neurobiologist: A scientist who studies the nervous system.

Neuroendocrinologist: A scientist who studies the interaction between the nervous system and the endocrine (or glandular) system.

Neuropsychologist: A scientist who studies the influence of the nervous system on behavior.

O

Ornithologist: A scientist who studies birds.

P

Patent: A document granting an inventor the right to make, use, or sell an invention.

Physicist: A scientist who studies the interaction between energy and matter.

Primatologist: A scientist who studies apes and monkeys, as well as smaller primates such as lemurs and tarsiers.

Prime minister: The chief minister of a country.

Psychologist: A scientist who studies the human mind and behavior.

R

Renaiassance: The transitional movement between medieval and modern times, beginning in Italy in the fourteenth century and lasting into the seventeenth century; a period marked by a revival of classical arts and literature and the beginnings of modern science.

Revolution: Major political, social, or cultural change.

Roman Catholicism: the faith, practice, and system of the ancient Christian church.

S

Saint: A person who has been officially recognized by a religious body (such as the Catholic Church) as being holy and therefore worthy of public veneration, or worship.

Suffrage: The right to vote; a suffragette is a woman who advocates the right to vote for women.

T

Temperance: The use of moderation or self-restraint in personal activities, such as eating or drinking; also the name given to the movement that advocated moderation in and abstinence (total avoidance) from alcohol compumption.

Z

Zoologist: A biologist who studies and classifies animal life.

Media

Magazines
Newspapers
Television
Prize Winners
Miscellaneous

Magazines

1828 ▪ Sarah Josepha Hale (1788-1879), an American writer, was the first female editor of *Ladies' Magazine,* the first periodical for women in the United States. When the magazine's publishing headquarters moved to Philadelphia in 1837, the magazine title changed to *Godey's Lady's Book.* By 1860 it had the largest circulation for a magazine of its kind in America. In addition to her association with the magazine, Hale also published *Dictionary of Poetical Quotations, The Ladies' Wreath* (a collection of works by English and American women writers), *Women's Record* (a collection of biographies of notable women), and many other works.

Source: Read, Phyllis J., and Bernard L. Witlieb, *The Book of Women's Firsts.* New York: Random House, 1992, pp. 190-91.

1867 ▪ Mary Louise Booth (1831-1889), an American writer, was the first person to serve as editor of *Harper's Bazaar.*

Barbara Walters was the first female co-anchor of an evening news program. (See "Television" entry dated 1976.)

Based in New York City, the magazine was initially a 16-page family weekly published especially for women. *Harper's Bazaar* featured fashion news and stories by British and American authors. By 1877 the magazine had a circulation of 80,000.

Source: James, Edward T., and others, *Notable American Women, 1607-1950: A Biographical Dictionary,* Cambridge, Massachusetts: Harvard University Press, 1971, pp. 207-08.

1892 ▪ **Hind Nawfal,** an Egyptian journalist, founded *al-Fatah* ("The Young Woman"), the first women's magazine in Egypt. Calling the publication the "first of its kind under the Eastern sky," Nawfal promised to "adorn its pages with pearls from the pens of women." *al-Fatah* was the first of many Arabic women's magazines in Egypt, which came to be known as *al-majallat al-nisa'iyya* ("women's journals").

Source: Baron, Beth, *The Women's Awakening in Egypt: Culture, Society, and the Press.* New Haven/London: Yale University Press, 1994, pp. 1, 14.

1926 ▪ **Marie Mattingly Meloney** (1878-1943), an American magazine editor, was the first editor of *This Week* magazine. *This Week* began as a Sunday supplement to the *Herald Tribune,* a newspaper published in New York City. By 1935 *This Week* was distributed nationally as a Sunday supplement in newspapers throughout the country. Meloney was in charge of the magazine until her death. She was also remembered for raising $100,000 to buy a gram of radium for researcher Marie Curie (1867-1934) to use in cancer studies. In 1921 Meloney brought Curie to the United States to receive the radium.

Source: O'Neill, Lois Decker, ed., *The Women's Book of World Records and Achievements.* Garden City, New York: Doubleday, 1979, p. 442.

1945 ▪ **Hélène Gordon-Lazareff** (1909-1988), a Russian-born French journalist, and the French journalist **Françoise Giroud** founded the famous fashion magazine *Elle.* Gordon-Lazareff served as editor until 1973.

Source: Uglow, Jennifer S., ed., *The Continuum Dictionary of Women's Biography.* New York: Continuum, 1989, p. 232.

c. 1970 ▪ **Amanah Al-Sa`id** (1914-1995), an Egyptian journalist, was the first woman elected to the Egyptian Press Syndicate Executive Board. Al-Sa`id was the editor of *Hawã* ("Eve"), a woman's weekly magazine that had the largest foreign circulation of any Arabic paper. Al-Sa`id was also president of Dar al Hilal Publishing House, the oldest publisher in the Arab world.

Source: Parry, Melanie, ed., *Larousse Dictionary of Women.* New York: Continuum, 1995, p. 18.

1971 ▪ **Gloria Steinem** (1934-), an American writer and feminist, cofounded *Ms. Magazine* with Patricia Carbine in New York City. In 1971 Steinem also helped found the National Women's Political Caucus and the Women's Action Alliance to promote women's rights and fight discrimination. In addition to writing for *Ms.* and other journals, Steinem published several books, including *Outrageous Acts and Everyday Rebellions* (1983), *Revolution from Within: A Book of Self-Esteem* (1992), and *Moving Beyond Words* (1994).

Source: Magnusson, Magnus, *Larousse Biographical Dictionary.* Edinburgh: Larousse Kingfisher Chambers, Inc., 1994, p. 1392.

1982 ▪ **Lisa Henson,** daughter of famed puppeteer Jim Henson, was appointed the first female president of *The Harvard Lampoon,* a humor journal published at Harvard University. Graduating with a major in ancient Greek folklore and mythology, Henson went on to become president of Columbia Pictures in 1994.

Source: *The New York Times.* April 4, 1994.

1996 ▪ **Cathleen Black,** an American magazine executive, became the first female president of Hearst Magazines. Black was also appointed head of the Hearst publications *Cosmopolitan, Redbook, Harper's Bazaar,* and *Esquire.* Black had a long career in magazine publishing. She was involved in the launching of *Ms. Magazine* in 1971, and she became the first woman publisher of *New York* magazine in 1979. Four years later Black was appointed president of the newspaper *USA Today,* later becoming the newspaper's publisher (chief executive officer, or CEO). Black was elected the first female president of the Newspaper Association of America in 1991.

Source: *Working Woman.* November/December, 1996.

Newspapers

1831 ▪ Anne Newport Royall (1769-1854) was the first American newspaperwoman. Beginning her career as a travel writer and novelist, Royall published her first newspaper, *Paul Pry* (a weekly gossip sheet), in Washington, D.C. Five years later Royall started a new paper, *The Huntress,* which she continued to edit until 1854.

Source: James, Edward T., and others, *Notable American Women, 1607-1950: A Biographical Dictionary,* Cambridge, Massachusetts: Harvard University Press, 1971, pp. 204-05.

1868 ▪ Myra Colby Bradwell (1831-1894), an American journalist, founded the *Chicago Legal News.* A special charter was granted to free Bradwell from her status as a dependent married woman so she could serve as both proprietor (owner) and manager of the publication, which printed official court reports. Bradwell managed the *Chicago Legal News* until her death; Bradwell's daughter continued her mother's work until 1925.

Source: Uglow, Jennifer S., ed., *The Continuum Dictionary of Women's Biography.* New York: Continuum, 1989, p. 85.

c. 1880 ▪ Mary Ann Shadd Cary (1823-1893), a Canadian journalist, was the first African-American newspaperwoman. Publisher of Canada's first anti-slavery newspaper, *The Provincial Freeman,* Cary also became the second African-American woman to earn a law degree in the United States.

Source: James, Edward T., and others, *Notable American Women, 1607-1950: A Biographical Dictionary.* Cambridge, Massachusetts: Harvard University Press, 1971, pp. 300-01.

1897 ▪ **Marguerite Durand** (1864-1936), a French journalist, founded *La Fronde* ("The Insurrectionist"), the world's first daily newspaper for women. Durand was the co-director of *Les Nouvelles* ("The News"), a Parisian evening newspaper, from 1908 until 1914.

Source: Uglow, Jennifer S., ed., *The Continuum Dictionary of Women's Biography.* New York: Continuum, 1989, pp. 178-79.

1897 ▪ **Motoko Hani** (1873-1957), a Japanese journalist and educator, was the first female newspaper reporter in Japan. While working for the newspaper *Hochi Shimbun* in Tokyo, Hani covered women, education, and religion. Later she and her husband, Yoshikazu Hani, published *Fujin no Tomo,* a popular women's magazine. In 1921 the couple founded a liberal private school called Jiyu Gakuen. Motoko Hani was the school's first female principal.

Source: Uglow, Jennifer S., ed., *The Continuum Dictionary of Women's Biography.* New York: Continuum, 1989, p. 247.

1900 ▪ **Winifred Sweet Black** (1863-1936), an American journalist, was the first woman to write an account of the tidal wave that killed over 7,000 people in Galveston, Texas. Black dressed as a boy so she could get through police lines and cover the event. Associated throughout her career with the sensationalist newspapers published by William Randolph Hearst (1863-1951), Black was also the first woman to report on a prize fight.

Source: James, Edward T., and others, *Notable American Women, 1607-1950: A Biographical Dictionary.* Cambridge, Massachusetts: Harvard University Press, 1971, pp. 154-56.

1914 ▪ **Louella Oettinger Parsons** (1893-1972), an American reporter, wrote the first movie column to appear in a major American newspaper. Parsons's daily reports of gossip about the lives of movie stars ran in the *Chicago Herald* from 1914 through 1918. The column was syndicated shortly thereafter, and by the 1930s and 1940s it was carried by over 400 newspapers. Parsons retired in 1965.

Source: Acker, Ally, *Reel Women: Pioneers of the Cinema, 1896 to the Present.* New York: Continuum, 1991, pp. 332-33.

Sigma Delta Chi Admitted Women

In 1969 Sigma Delta Chi, an American society dedicated to the promotion of excellence in journalism, accepted female members for the first time in the organization's 60-year history. Among the sixteen women admitted was an African American reporter, **Charlayne Hunter** (later Gault), who wrote for *The New York Times.*

1915 ▪ Mary Roberts Rinehart (1876-1958), an American writer, was the first American news correspondent to report from the battlefront during World War I (1914-1918). Rinehart sent back news articles for the *Saturday Evening Post* from the trenches in France and Belgium in 1915. Perhaps best known as a mystery writer, Rinehart published such classic detective novels as *The Circular Staircase* (1908), *The Man in Lower Ten* (1909), and *Tish* (1920).

Source: Read, Phyllis J., and Bernard L. Witlieb, *The Book of Women's Firsts.* New York: Random House, 1992, pp. 372-73.

1930 ▪ Eleanor Medill Patterson (1881-1948), an American journalist, was the first woman to publish a daily newspaper in Washington, D.C. After becoming restless with her life as a wealthy socialite, Patterson persuaded her friend, newspaper publisher William Randolph Hearst (1863-1951), to let her take over the *Washington Herald.* Although she had no experience in running a newspaper, she came from a family of journalists. Proving her shrewd business sense, within a few years Patterson raised the circulation of the floundering *Herald.* By 1937 she had also taken over the Hearst evening paper, the *Washington Times.* Two years later she bought both newspapers and merged them into the *Washington Times- Herald.*

Source: James, Edward T., and others, *Notable American Women, 1607-1950: A Biographical Dictionary,* Cambridge, Massachusetts: Harvard University Press, 1971, pp. 26-29.

1935 ▪ Esther Van Wagoner Tufty (1896-1986), an American journalist, founded Tufty News Service in Washington, D.C. The service provided political coverage for Michigan newspapers. Tufty served the organization as president, editor, and writer from 1935 to 1985. In 1971 she became the first woman elected to the National Press Club, in honor of her long career and for establishing Tufty News Service.

Source: Read, Phyllis J., and Bernard L. Witlieb, *The Book of Women's Firsts.* New York: Random House, 1992, pp. 452-53.

1942 ▪ **Margaret Petherbridge Farrar** (1897-1984) became the first editor of the *The New York Times* crossword puzzle on February 15, 1942. In 1924 Faffar wrote—with F. G. Hartswick and Prosper Buranelli—the first book of crossword puzzles. A 1919 graduate of Smith College, Farrar married John Farrar, cofounder of the publishing house of Farrar, Strauss & Giroux, in 1926.

Source: Read, Phyllis J., and Bernard L. Witlieb, *The Book of Women's Firsts*. New York: Random House, 1992, pp. 149-50.

1966 ▪ **Charlotte Curtis** (c.1928-1987), an American journalist, was the first woman whose name was placed on the masthead (list of owners and editors) of the *The New York Times*. Joining the newspaper as a reporter in 1961, Curtis served as editor of the "Family/Style" section from 1966 until 1974. She then became associate editor of the newspaper and an editor of the opinion-editorial page. Curtis focused on serious women's issues, refusing to let trivial news dominate the "society" section and setting a trend that was followed by newspapers throughout the country.

Journalist Helen A. Thomas was the first woman to head the White House bureau of a major news service.

Source: O'Neill, Lois Decker, *The Women's Book of World Records and Achievements*. Garden City, New York: Doubleday, 1979, pp. 466-67.

1974 ▪ **Helen A. Thomas** (1920-), an American journalist, was the first woman to head the White House bureau of a major news service. Appointed White House bureau chief for United Press International in 1974, Thomas held the position for over two decades.

Source: Read, Phyllis J., and Bernard L. Witlieb, *The Book of Women's Firsts*. New York: Random House, 1992, pp. 441-42.

1975 ▪ **Robin Herman,** an American journalist, became the first woman sportswriter for *The New York Times*. Joining a staff of 51 men, Herman reported primarily on professional hockey. After being on the job for awhile, Herman found she could not interview players because she was barred from entering team dressing rooms. Waging a campaign for equal treatment with male journalists, Herman finally gained access to the New York Rangers' locker rooms.

Source: O'Neill, Lois Decker, *The Women's Book of World Records and Achievements*. Garden City, New York: Doubleday, 1979, p. 463.

Television

1947 ▪ Dorothy Fuldheim (1893-1989) became the first female television news anchor. She was appointed to the position at WEWS-TV in Cleveland, Ohio. At first, the beer company that sponsored the nightly newscast was reluctant to back a program featuring a woman. The station, which was the largest between New York City and Chicago, Illinois, stood by Fuldheim. Eventually the beer company relented, entering into a sponsorship that lasted for 18 years. In 1979, at age 86, Fuldheim was still anchoring the early newscast in Cleveland, earning the distinction of being on the job longer than any other television broadcaster.

Source: McCullough, Joan, *First of All: Significant "Firsts" by American Women*. New York: Holt, 1980, pp. 33-34.

1972 ▪ Rachel Flint Heyhoe (1939-), an English cricket player, was the first female sports reporter for Independent Television in Britain. Heyhoe also served as vice chair of the Women's Cricket Association from 1981 to 1986.

Source: Uglow, Jennifer S., ed., *The Continuum Dictionary of Women's Biography*. New York: Continuum, 1989, p. 258.

1976 ▪ Barbara Walters (1931-), an American television newscaster, was the first female co-anchor of an evening news program. Hired by the American Broadcasting Company (ABC-TV), Walters worked with Harry Reasoner on the *ABC Evening News* from 1976 to 1978. Walters began her 14-year career with the National Broadcasting Company (NBC-TV) in 1961 as a

Dorothy Fuldheim was the first female television news anchor. Fuldheim was still anchoring an early newscast at age 86.

writer for the *Today Show*. When she left NBC in 1976, she was co-host of the morning show. After joining ABC Walters became famous for her interviews with celebrities on *The Barbara Walters Specials* and for the special issues program *20/20*, which she has co-hosted with Hugh Downs since 1979.

Source: Read, Phyllis J., and Bernard L. Witlieb, *The Book of Women's Firsts.* New York: Random House, 1992, pp. 468-69.

1987 ▪ **Gayle Sierens** (1954-), an American television sports-caster, was the first woman to do play-by-play coverage of a National Football League game. On December 27, 1987, Sierens reported on the game between the Kansas City Chiefs and the Seattle Seahawks for the National Broadcasting Company (NBC-TV) television network.

Source: Read, Phyllis J., and Bernard L. Witlieb, *The Book of Women's Firsts.* New York: Random House, 1992, p. 408.

1993 ▪ **Lucie Salhany** (1946-), an American television executive, was the first woman to head a national television network. Salhany was named chair of Fox Broadcasting in Hollywood, California. Following a dispute with Fox owner Rupert Murdoch, Salhany left the network in 1994 after 18 months on the job.

Source: *Newsweek.* July 18, 1994, p. 65.

1977 ▪ **Kay Koplovitz,** an American cable-television executive, founded the USA Network. Few women were working in the cable industry when Koplovitz started a cable service she devised to reach family viewers with an assortment of shows. The change of format from all sports to family entertainment resulted in quick growth and high profits.

The USA Network eventually became the top-rated basic cable network in prime time (the evening hours of 7:00-11:00 p.m. when most people watch television). Koplovitz eventually expanded the service abroad to Latin America, Europe, and South America. The successful Sci-Fi (Science Fiction) channel was added with its own Web site, called "The Dominion," on the Internet (a worldwide computer network). Koplovitz predicted that personal computers will replace televisions in the future, and she is investigating ways to link cable television with the Internet.

Source: Karlin, Sue, "Kay Koplovitz: First Woman to Head her Own Cable-TV Channel," *Working Woman.* November/December, 1996, p. 109.

1978 ▪ **Jane Cahill Pfeiffer** (1932-), an American executive, was the first woman to serve as chair of the board of the

National Broadcasting Company (NBC-TV). She held the position from 1978 until 1980. Pfeiffer has been active throughout her life in business and public service.

Source: Read, Phyllis J., and Bernard L. Witlieb, *The Book of Women's Firsts.* New York: Random House, 1992, pp. 343-44.

c. 1986 ▪ Oprah Winfrey (1954-), an American television entertainer and executive, became the first woman to own and produce a talk show; she was also the first African American to own a major television studio. Winfrey began her career at a television station in Nashville, Tennessee. Moving to Baltimore, Maryland, in 1977, Winfrey was co-host of *Baltimore is Talking* until 1984, when she took a similar position in Chicago, Illinois. Originally titled *A.M. Chicago,* her program soon became *The Oprah Winfrey Show,* featuring audience participation in discussions of controversial issues. By 1986 Winfrey was one of the most famous women in television, daily reaching seventeen million viewers who responded enthusiastically to her wit and open personality.

Winfrey also showed talent as an actress, gaining an Academy Award nomination for her performance in the film *The Color Purple* (1985), which was based on the novel by Alice Walker. In 1997 Winfrey premiered an evening television program called *Dinner With Oprah,* in which she talked with writers about literature. Winfrey was inducted into the Women's Hall of Fame in 1994.

Source: Parry, Melanie, ed., *Larousse Dictionary of Women.* New York: Larousse Kingfisher Chambers, Inc. 1995, p. 695.

1996 ▪ Jamie Tarses, (1963?-), an American television executive, was the first female president of a major television network division. Tarses achieved this distinction when she was appointed president of the television entertainment division at the American Broadcasting Company (ABC-TV) in 1996. The daughter of Hollywood TV producer Jat Tarses, Jamie grew up learning about the inside world of television writing and producing. Before moving to ABC, Jamie Tarses had worked in television program development at the National Broadcasting

Company (NBC-TV), where she was involved in the production of such shows as *Friends, Frasier,* and *Caroline in the City.*

Source: Seger, Linda, "Jamie Tarses: First Woman President of a Major TV Network Division," *Working Woman.* November/December, 1996.

Prize Winners

1937 ▪ **Anne O'Hare McCormick** (1880-1954), an American journalist, was the first woman to receive the Pulitzer Prize for distinguished correspondence. She was honored for her reports on international affairs at *The New York Times.* In 1936 McCormick had also become the first woman to serve on the *Times* editorial board.

Source: Read, Phyllis J., and Bernard L. Witlieb, *The Book of Women's Firsts.* New York: Random House, 1992, pp. 278-79.

1949 ▪ **Shirley Dinsdale** (1928-), an American puppeteer, became the first woman to win an Emmy award. (The Emmy is an award given by the television industry.) Dinsdale was recognized as "most outstanding television personality" for her work on her puppet show *Judy Splinters* in 1949. Starting a show business career at age 15, Dinsdale trained with the famous ventriloquist Edgar Bergen (1903-1978; a ventriloquist is a performer who can make his or her voice seem to be coming from another source, usually a puppet). Dinsdale had her own radio program when she was 17.

Source: Read, Phyllis J., and Bernard L. Witlieb, *The Book of Women's Firsts.* New York: Random House, 1992, p. 122.

1951 ▪ **Marguerite Higgins** (1920-1966), an American journalist, was the first woman to win the Pulitzer Prize for international reporting. She was honored with fellow reporter Homer Bigart for their coverage of the Korean War (1950-1953) for the *New York Herald Tribune.* The only woman reporting from the battlefront in Korea, Higgins had also reported from the war zone during World War II (1939-1945). She later covered the Vietnam War (1954-1975).

Source: Read, Phyllis J., and Bernard L. Witlieb, *The Book of Women's Firsts.* New York: Random House, 1992, pp. 202-03.

1954 ▪ **Virginia M. Schau** (1915-1989), an amateur photographer, was the first woman to receive a Pulitzer Prize for spot news photography. She was honored for the photographs she took of her husband, Walter, during his rescue of a truck driver from a crash near Redding, California. The Schau family were traveling in their car behind the truck on a bridge when the truck's steering mechanism failed. As the truck broke through

The only woman to file reports from the battlefront in Korea, Marguerite Higgins was also known for her "front line" coverage of World War II.

a guard rail, the engine caught fire and the cab came to a stop, teetering on the edge of the bridge by its rear wheels. Virginia Schau took photographs as Walter Schau, his feet held by other people at the scene, hung from the bridge and used a rope to pull the driver from the burning cab.

Source: Read, Phyllis J., and Bernard L. Witlieb, *The Book of Women's Firsts.* New York: Random House, 1992, pp. 393-94.

1964 ▪ **Hazel Brannon Smith** (1914-1994), an American journalist, was the first woman to be awarded the Pulitzer Prize for editorial writing. She was honored for her work in the *Lexington Advertiser,* one of two newspapers she owned in Lexington, Mississippi. Throughout her journalism career Smith campaigned against political corruption and racism, in spite of lawsuits and boycotts brought against her by people who opposed her views.

Source: Read, Phyllis J., and Bernard L. Witlieb, *The Book of Women's Firsts.* New York: Random House, 1992, pp. 410-11.

1971 ▪ **Lucinda Franks** (1946-), an American journalist, was the first woman to win the Pulitzer Prize for national reporting; she was also the youngest person ever to receive the award. Franks shared the Pulitzer with Thomas Powers for the duo's five-article series, "The Making of a Terrorist," about Diana Oughton, a New York socialite who became a political activist. Oughton was killed in an explosion in a home in the Greenwich Village section of New York City, where bombs were reportedly being manufactured.

Source: O'Neill, Lois Decker, *The Women's Book of World Records and Achievements.* Garden City, New York: Doubleday, 1979, p. 465.

1975 ▪ **Mary McGrory** (1918-), an American journalist, was the first woman to receive a Pulitzer Prize for commentary. She was honored for her political journalism in a syndicated column. During the 1950s McGrory covered congressional hearings chaired by Senator Joseph McCarthy (1908-1957), who headed a campaign to identify suspected communists in the United States government and the entertainment industry. In the early 1970s she reported on the Watergate scandal, which involved an illegal burglary of the Democratic Party headquarters by associates of Republican President Richard M. Nixon (served in office 1969-1974).

Source: Read, Phyllis J., and Bernard L. Witlieb, *The Book of Women's Firsts*. New York: Random House, 1992, p. 282.

Miscellaneous

1939 ▪ Pauline Frederick (1906-1990), an American journalist, was the first woman to work as a radio network news analyst and diplomatic correspondent in the United States. Frederick made her first national broadcast from Washington, D.C., in 1939 and her first overseas broadcast, from China, five years later. Frederick was also a pioneer in television, becoming the first woman to anchor coverage of a presidential convention in 1960. She was the United Nations correspondent for the National Broadcasting Company (NBC-TV) for twenty-one years.

Source: Read, Phyllis J., and Bernard L. Witlieb, *The Book of Women's Firsts*. New York: Random House, 1992, p. 167.

1941 ▪ Margaret Bourke-White (1904-1971), an American photojournalist, was the first woman to serve as a photographer for the U.S. armed forces. Attached to the Third U.S. Army under General George Patton during World War II (1939-1945), she photographed the German attack on Moscow, Russia, in 1941. She also covered combat in North Africa and Italy. Bourke-White was one of the first photographers to enter the Nazi concentration camps in 1944. Her pictures of the camp at Buchenwald, Germany, provoked worldwide outrage.

Source: Magnusson, Magnus, *Larousse Biographical Dictionary*. Edinburgh: Larousse Kingfisher Chambers, Inc., 1994, p. 189.

c. 1950s ▪ Pauline Kael (1919-) was the first American woman to establish a reputation as a serious film critic. Her

Brenda Starr

In 1940 Dale Messick, an American cartoonist, became the first woman to create and publish a syndicated comic strip. Her *Brenda Starr* comic strip, which she published in the *Chicago Tribune,* was also notable for being the first comic strip to feature a woman. While trying to find a publisher for her cartoons, Messick changed her name from Dalia to Dale to conceal the fact that she was a woman.

reviewing career began in the 1950s while she managed two art film theaters in Berkeley, California. From 1968 to 1991 Kael was the movie critic (she prefers the term "movie") for the *New Yorker*. The author of numerous collections of reviews, Kael was one of the most popular critics in the history of film.

Source: Magnusson, Magnus, *Larousse Biographical Dictionary*. Edinburgh: Larousse Kingfisher Chambers, Inc., 1994, p. 804.

1970 ▪ **Sally Aw Sian** (1931-), a Chinese journalist, was the first woman to chair the International Press Institute in Hong Kong. Sian held the post from 1970 to 1971. She was also the founder and first chair of the Chinese Language Press Institute.

Source: O'Neill, Lois Decker, *The Women's Book of World Records and Achievements*. Garden City, New York: Doubleday, 1979, p. 465.

1976 ▪ **Alison Steele** (1938-1995), professionally known as the "Night Bird," was the first woman named *Billboard* FM (radio) Personality of the Year. (*Billboard* is a music industry magazine that publishes ratings of recent popular recordings according to sales.) A disc jockey (DJ) for WNEW-FM in New York City, Steele had developed a tremendous following on her late night show. Like the other DJs during the late 1960s and the 1970s, she kept listeners informed about rapid social change through what was called a free-form or progressive format.

Source: *The New York Times*. October 29, 1995.

1992 ▪ **Dee Dee Myers** (1961-), an American journalist, was the first woman appointed as White House press secretary. After working as President Bill Clinton's campaign spokeswoman, Meyers was the White House press secretary from 1992 to 1994.

Source: *The New York Times*. December 24, 1992.

Professions

Architecture
Law Enforcement
Law
Medicine and Health
Military

Architecture

1869 ▪ Harriet Morrison Irwin (1828-1897), an American architect, was the first woman in the United States to patent (license a design under one's own name) an architectural innovation. A self-trained architect, Irwin received a patent for her design for a hexagonal (six-sided) house in Charlotte, North Carolina.

Source: Vare, Ethlie Ann, and Greg Ptacek, *Mothers of Invention: From the Bra to the Bomb, Forgotten Women and Their Unforgettable Ideas.* New York: William Morrow, 1988, pp. 165-66.

1890 ▪ Louise Blanchard Bethune (1856-1913) was the first woman to become a professional architect in the United States. After opening an independent office in Buffalo, New York, in 1881, Bethune was elected to a full membership in the American Institute of Architects in 1890. Bethune's designs included schools in New York state, factories, housing projects, and banks.

Belva Ann Bennett McNall Lockwood was the first woman allowed to present arguments before the U.S. Supreme Court. (See "Law" entry dated 1879.)

Source: James, Edward T., and others, *Notable American Women, 1607-1950: A Biographical Dictionary.* Cambridge, Massachusetts: Harvard University Press, 1971, pp. 140-41.

1907 ▪ Louise Caldwell Murdock (1858-1915), an American interior designer, was the first woman to design and build a fireproof office building. (An interior designer coordinates wallcoverings, draperies, furniture, and other accessories in the rooms of a house or building.) Murdock had a distinguished professional career. Educated at the New York School of Fine and Applied Art, she stressed simple interior design and proportions in her work. Murdock also concentrated on the harmonious and functional relationship between a house and the surrounding landscape.

Source: James, Edward T., and others, *Notable American Women, 1607-1950: A Biographical Dictionary.* Cambridge, Massachusetts: Harvard University Press, 1971, pp. 601-02.

1948 ▪ Sylvia Crowe (1901-), a British landscape architect, cofounded the International Federation of Landscape Architects. (A landscape architect designs gardens, lawns, and other features of the outdoor area that surrounds a house or building.) Known for designing new town landscapes, Crowe wrote such influential book as *Tomorrow's Landscape* (1956) and *Gardens of Moghul India* (1972).

Source: Uglow, Jennifer S., *The Continuum Dictionary of Women's Biography.* New York: Continuum, 1989, p. 141.

1954 ▪ Norma Merrick Sklarek (1928-), an American architect, was the first African-American woman to register as an architect. Obtaining her license in New York state in 1954, Sklarek went on to become the first African-American female fellow of the American Institute of Architects in 1980.

Source: Smith, Jessie Carney, *Black Firsts: 2,000 Years of Extraordinary Achievement.* Detroit: Gale Research, 1994, p. 1.

1962 ▪ Brenda Colvin (1897-1981), a British landscape architect, designed Gale Common. (A landscape architect designs gardens, lawns, and other features of the outdoor area that surrounds a house or building.) Colvin created the imaginative landscape, which utilized waste ashes left from burnt coal, while working for the British government. A cofounder of the Institute of Landscape Architects in 1929, she wrote the classic book *Land and Landscape* (1947).

Source: Uglow, Jennifer S., *The Continuum Dictionary of Women's Biography.* New York: Continuum, 1989, pp. 133-34.

"Atelier 66"

In 1965 **Suzana Maria Antonakakis** (1935-), a Greek architect, cofounded "Atelier 66" with her husband, Dimitris Antonakakis. One of the leading development firms in Greece, "Atelier 66" specialized in designing new structures and restoring old buildings.

Law Enforcement

1910 ▪ **Alice Stebbins Wells** (1873-?), an American police officer, was the first woman in the United States to receive a regular appointment as a police officer. After successfully taking the civil service exam, Wells performed patrol functions with the power to arrest in Los Angeles, California. (Service exams are standardized tests required for employment at many civil and government jobs.) By 1914 three other women had joined the force, and the four officers were assigned to movie theaters and skating rinks and investigated cases involving abandoned women. Wells retired after a 30-year career.

Source: Read, Phyllis J., and Bernard L. Witlieb, *The Book of Women's Firsts.* New York: Random House, 1992, pp. 474-75.

1972 ▪ **Joanne E. Pierce** (1941-) and **Susan Lynn Roley** (1947-), American law enforcement officials, were the first two women to serve as special agents of the Federal Bureau of Investigation (FBI). The women passed a rigorous course at Quantico, Virginia, in 1972. The predecessor of the FBI, called the Bureau of Investigation, hired its first female agent in 1911. When J. Edgar Hoover (1895-1972) became head of the FBI, however, he forbade the hiring of female agents. Since his death in 1972, however, women have regularly served as agents.

Source: Read, Phyllis J., and Bernard L. Witlieb, *The Book of Women's Firsts.* New York: Random House, 1992, pp. 347-48.

1979 ▪ **Eloise Randolf Page,** an American intelligence officer, was the first female station chief (head of a main office or bureau) in the Central Intelligence Agency (CIA). Page's intelligence career began after World War II (1939-1945), when the CIA was called the OSS (Office of Strategic Services). During her 40 years in the CIA, Page was the first branch chief, first division chief, and first station chief. She was also the first woman in the Directorate of Operations, the clandestine (secret) wing of the CIA.

Source: *Working Woman.* November/December, 1996, p. 58.

1985 ▪ Penny Harrington (1943-), an American law enforcement official, was the first female to head the police department in a major American city. Harrington's tenure was short lived, however, because she instituted controversial changes that angered the police union and other officials.

In one change that caused a great deal of controversy, Harrington barred the choke hold (a method used by police to restrain a crime suspect, which involves locking the suspect's neck in the crook of the policeman's arm). Replacing the terms "patrolman" and "policewoman" with "police officer," Harrington also posted job openings as equal-opportunity positions. As executive director of the National Center for Women and Policing, Harrington maintained that it takes ten years to make lasting changes in police departments in order to avoid tokenism (making appointments without regard to qualifications to meet a quota). She estimated that women should ideally comprise 25 percent of the police force.

Source: Read, Phyllis J., and Bernard L. Witlieb, *The Book of Women's Firsts.* New York: Random House, 1992, pp. 194-95.

Law

C. A.D. 100 ▪ Beruriah, an ancient Hebrew scholar and legal expert, is the first and only woman mentioned in the Talmud (a collection of ancient writings that form the basis for traditional Judaism). Beruriah wrote commentaries on the law, and when her husband tried to discredit her intellectual achievements by challenging her sexual fidelity, she killed herself.

Source: Chicago, Judy, *The Dinner Party*. New York: Anchor, 1979, p. 118.

1869 ▪ Arabella Aurelia Babb Mansfield

(1846-1911), an American lawyer, was the first female lawyer admitted to the bar (to be licensed to practice law). She received a law degree from Iowa Wesleyan University in 1866 along with her husband, John Mansfield. He immediately became a member of the bar, but by strict interpretation of the Iowa Code—which stated that "any white male person" could become a member of the bar—Arabella Mansfield did not have the same right. Arabella Mansfield argued her own case before Judge Francis Springer. The judge finally issued an interpretation of the statute language to mean that "the affirmative declaration [for males] is not a denial of the right of females." It would be another three years before the statute was officially amended to specifically allow women to be admitted to the bar.

Deborah the Judge

Deborah is the only female judge mentioned in the Scriptures. The only woman of her time to possess political power through popular consent, Deborah was also a prophet (a person who can predict future events). She was the only judge to perform prophetic functions before Samuel, a prophet and the last judge of Israel. The "Song of Deborah" is the most ancient piece of literature in the Hebrew Bible.

Source: James, Edward T., and others, *Notable American Women, 1607-1950: A Biographical Dictionary*. Cambridge, Massachusetts: Harvard University Press, 1971, pp. 492-93.

1872 ▪ Charlotte E. Ray

(1850-1911), an American lawyer, was the first African-American woman lawyer. After graduating from Howard University Law School in 1872, she was admitted to the bar (licensed to practice law) in Washington, D.C. Ray was the first African-American woman admitted to the bar in the United States, as well as the first woman admitted to the bar in the District of Columbia.

Source: James, Edward T., and others, *Notable American Women, 1607-1950: A Biographical Dictionary*. Cambridge, Massachusetts: Harvard University Press, 1971, pp. 121-22.

1879 ▪ Belva Ann Bennett McNall Lockwood

(1830-1917), an American lawyer, was the first woman admitted to practice before the U.S. Supreme Court. She attained this distinction when she succeeded in lobbying for a bill that permitted women to argue cases before the nation's highest court. President Rutherford B. Hayes (served in office from 1877-1881) signed the bill on February 15, 1879, and the following month Lockwood was admitted to practice. In both 1884 and 1888, she was nominated for president of the United States by the National Equal Rights Party, winning over four thousand votes. Lockwood was an ardent pacifist (a person who opposes violence, especially warfare) and served as a member of the nominating committee for the Nobel Peace Prize. She worked until age 76, successfully arguing a claim for the Eastern Cherokee Indians that brought the tribe an award of $5 million.

Source: Chicago, Judy, *The Dinner Party*. New York: Anchor, 1979, p. 192.

1893 ▪ Cornelia Sorabji (1866-1954), an Indian lawyer, became the first woman in her country to practice law. She was educated at Decca College in Poona, India, where she was the first female student, as well as at Gujarat College and Sommerville College, Oxford. By special Congregational Decree in 1893, Sorabji was the first woman allowed to sit for the advanced examination in civil law at Oxford. (This was 30 years before women in England were allowed to be licensed to practice law, which is known as being "admitted to the bar.") Sorabji later returned to India to practice law. By 1904 she was appointed as legal advisor on behalf of women in *purdah* in Bihar, Orissa, and Assam. (Purdah is a Muslim and Hindu religious law that requires women to secluded.) In 1923 Sorabji settled in Calcutta to practice as a barrister (courtroom lawyer).

Source: Uglow, Jennifer S., ed., *The Continuum Dictionary of Women's Biography*. New York: Continuum, 1989, p. 508.

1916 ▪ Emily Gowan Murphy (1868-1933), a Canadian lawyer, was the first female magistrate (judge) in the British Empire. In 1916 she was appointed to the juvenile court where she served until her retirement in 1931. Murphy worked to establish a special court to hear "difficult cases" (such as sexual assault) and was instrumental in bringing into being the Women's Court (established in 1916).

Source: Uglow, Jennifer S., ed., *The Continuum Dictionary of Women's Biography.* New York: Continuum, 1989, pp. 392-93.

1919 ▪ Helena Florence Normanton (1883-1957), a British lawyer, was the first woman accepted by the Inns of Court (the four legal societies that control admission to the bar, or the right to practice law) in London, England. She was also the first woman elected to the General Council of the Bar and one of the first women to be made a King's Counsel (lawyer to the monarchy) in England, both in 1949. Normanton had a distinguished career in law and worked for women's legal rights.

Source: Uglow, Jennifer S., ed., *The Continuum Dictionary of Women's Biography.* New York: Continuum, 1989, pp. 405-06.

Bolin Became Judge

Jane Matilda Bolin (1908-), an American lawyer, was the first African-American woman to become a judge in the United States. After earning a law degree at Yale University Law School, Bolin entered private practice. In 1939 she was appointed a judge in the Court of Domestic Relations in New York City, which later became the Family Court of the State of New York. Bolin served continuously in that position until her retirement; she also contributed to civil rights and other social causes.

1920 ▪ Florence Ellinwood Allen (1884-1966) was the first woman to serve as a judge in the United States. A graduate of New York University Law School, Ellinwood was elected common pleas court judge in Cleveland, Ohio, in 1920. Two years later she became the first woman elected to the Ohio Supreme Court, and in 1934 she became the first woman appointed to serve on the U.S. Court of Appeals.

Source: Read, Phyllis J., and Bernard L. Witlieb, *The Book of Women's Firsts.* New York: Random House, 1992, pp. 15-16.

1949 ▪ Bernita S. Matthews (1894-1988) was the first woman to serve as a U.S. federal district judge. Matthews was appointed to the federal District Court for the District of Columbia by President Harry S Truman (served in office 1945-1953) in 1949.

Source: Read, Phyllis J., and Bernard L. Witlieb, *The Book of Women's Firsts.* New York: Random House, 1992, p. 273.

c. 1950s ▪ **Angie Elizabeth Brooks-Randolph** (1928-), a Liberian lawyer, was the first woman to practice law in Liberia. She was also the first woman accepted as a legal apprentice in that country. Educated in the United States and England, Brooks-Randolph earned a law degree in London and was the second woman to serve as president of the United Nations General Assembly, a position she assumed in 1969. She was also the first woman in her country to hold a cabinet post (an appointed position high in the government). Brooks-Randolph earned an international reputation as an activist and a humanitarian.

Source: O'Neill, Lois Decker, ed., *The Women's Book of World Records and Achievements,* New York: Doubleday, 1979, pp. 64-65.

1962 ▪ **Marjorie McKensie Lawson** (1912-), an American lawyer, was the first African-American woman appointed to a judicial post by a U.S. president. A graduate of Terrell Law School and Columbia University School of Law, Lawson was named associate judge of the District of Columbia Juvenile Court by President John F. Kennedy (served in office from 1961-1963) in 1962. She held the post until 1965, when she was appointed to the United Nations Economic and Security Council's Social Commission (UNESCO). The following year President Lyndon B. Johnson (served in office 1963-1969) named Lawson a United States representative to the United Nations.

Source: *Negro Women in the Judiciary.* Chicago: Alpha Kappa Alpha Sorority, Inc., p. 13.

1965 ▪ **Elizabeth Lane** (1905-1988), an English lawyer, was the first female judge in England. In 1965 Lane was named to the High Court in the Family Division, a post she held until her retirement in 1979.

Source: Uglow, Jennifer S., ed., *The Continuum Dictionary of Women's Biography.* New York: Continuum, 1989, p. 311.

1995 ▪ **Roberta Cooper Ramo** (1942-), an attorney from Albuquerque, New Mexico, became the first female president of the American Bar Association (ABA; a professional association for American lawyers). Ramo was elected in Chicago, Illinois, at the ABA's annual meeting on August 9, 1995. In her acceptance speech, Ramo indicated that she hoped to use her position to provide legal services for the poor and help stop domestic abuse.

Source: *The New York Times.* August 11, 1995, p. A13.

In 1995 attorney Roberta Ramo became the first female president of the American Bar Association.

Medicine and Health

Seventh century B.C. ▪ Hygeia, a woman born in ancient Greece, was the first person to promote preventive medicine (medical procedures—such as check-ups, inoculations, and diet control—that help prevent disease or identify health risks before they become severe). It is from Hygeia's name that the word "hygiene" (a term referring to preventive practices that contribute to good health) comes from. According to legend, Hygeia was a descendant of the Asclepias, the Greek "physician to the gods."

Source: Levin, Beatrice, *Women and Medicine: Pioneers Meeting the Challenge!* Lincoln, Nebraska: Media Publishing, 1988, p. 75.

Fourth century B.C. ▪ Agnodice, a woman of ancient Greece, was the first female gynecologist (a doctor who treats the female reproductive system). Dressed in men's clothing, she studied with another doctor named Herophilos (c. 335-c. 280 B.C.). When Agnodice's female identity was revealed, she suffered the criticism of jealous colleagues.

Source: Ogilvie, Marilyn Bailey, *Women in Science: Antiquity through the Nineteenth Century.* Cambridge, Massachusetts: M.I.T. Press, 1986, p. 28.

C. A.D. 200 ▪ Metrodora, a physician living in second century Rome, wrote the oldest existing description of women's diseases and possible treatments. Metrodora prescribed various methods for dealing with diseases of the uterus (the womb), the stomach, and the kidneys.

Source: Chicago, Judy, *The Dinner Party.* New York: Anchor, 1979, p. 127.

A.D. 390 ▪ **Fabiola** (?-399), a Roman noblewoman, founded the first public hospital in Rome, Italy. Performing the services of nurse, physician, and surgeon, she also taught Christianity. With Christian scholars Paula, Eustochium, and the church father Jerome, Fabiola was an important figure in promoting a specifically female order of Christianity.

Source: Uglow, Jennifer S., ed., *The Continuum Dictionary of Women's Biography.* New York: Continuum, 1989, p. 195.

c. 1080 ▪ **Trotula of Salerno** (?-1097), an Italian physician and medical writer, was credited with a number of medical firsts. She was the first person to stitch a perineum (external tissue at the back of the genital canal) after a difficult childbirth. Trotula also introduced a means of supporting the perineum during labor to prevent it from tearing. She was best remembered for *Diseases of Women,* a book on gynecology (a branch of medicine specializing in disorders of the female reproductive system) and obstetrics (the care of women during pregnancy and after childbirth). Trotula's book remained an important medical reference work through the eighteenth century.

Source: Vare, Ethelie Ann, and Greg Ptacek, *Mothers of Invention: From the Bra to the Bomb, Forgotten Women and Their Unforgettable Ideas.* New York: William Morrow, 1988, pp. 27- 28.

c. 1100 ▪ **Queen Matilda** (c. 1100-1135), the wife of Henry I of England (1068-1135), founded a welfare program for pregnant women in need; she later established two free hospitals.

Source: Chicago, Judy, *The Dinner Party.* New York: Anchor, 1979, p. 143.

c. 1120 ▪ **Hildegard of Bingen** (1098-1178), a German nun, was one of the earliest German physicians. As abbess (head nun) of Rupertsberg Abbey, Hildegard wrote medical works on a number of topics, including descriptions of blood circulation and mental instability.

Source: Levin, Beatrice, *Women and Medicine: Pioneers Meeting the Challenge!* Lincoln, Nebraska: Media Publishing, 1988, p. 37.

c. 1320 ▪ **Alessandra Giliani** (1307-1326), an Italian anatomist (a person who studies the structure of the human body), was the first person to color veins and arteries in order to make them easier to see during medical examinations. Trained as a physician, Giliani developed a method of drawing blood from cadavers (dead bodies), then filling the veins and arteries with different colored liquids to make them more visible during autopsy (the examination of a body after death).

Source: Chicago, Judy, *The Dinner Party.* New York: Anchor, 1979, p. 154.

Sixteenth century ▪ **Marie Colinet,** a Swiss physician, was the first doctor to use a magnet to remove a piece of steel from a patient's eye. Historians have often mistakenly credited her husband—a fellow physician—with introducing this procedure.

Source: Chicago, Judy, *The Dinner Party.* New York: Anchor, 1979, p. 176.

c. 1600 ▪ **Louise Bourgeois** (1563-1636), a French midwife (a person who assists in the birth of babies), was the first person to treat anemia (a condition in which not enough oxygen is carried by the blood into body tissues) with iron. In 1608 she published a book on the anatomy (physical structure) and health of women and newborn babies. Bourgoeis also trained her daughter to be a midwife.

Source: Uglow, Jennifer S., ed., *The Continuum Dictionary of Women's Biography.* New York: Continuum, 1989, p. 82.

1718 ▪ **Mary Wortley Montagu** (1689-1762), an English traveler and writer, introduced smallpox variolation to England. (Smallpox is a highly contagious virus whose symptoms include high fever, vomiting, and infected lesions, or sores, that can cause scarring. "Variolation"—a primitive form of inoculation or injection—involved infecting healthy people with small amounts of smallpox. It was hoped that this would produce a mild form of the disease that would give the patient immunity from more serious strains.)

Mary Wortley Montagu, an English traveler and writer, introduced smallpox variolation to England.

Montagu had observed the practice during her stay in Constantinople, Turkey, where her husband was serving as ambassador from England. She promoted the technique despite heated opposition from the medical profession. The English government, skeptical of the procedure, appointed a four-physician panel to monitor its effects on the Montagu's own daughter.

When the experiment appeared to be a success, the panel reluctantly approved its use.

Source: Uglow, Jennifer S., ed., *The Continuum Dictionary of Women's Biography*. New York: Continuum, 1989, p. 385.

c. 1750 ▪ **Angelique du Coudray** (1712-1789), a French midwife (a person who assists in the birth of babies), introduced the use of a model of the female torso (upper body) and an actual fetus (an unborn infant in its later stages of development) when teaching obstetrics (the care of women during pregnancy and after delivery). Awarded an annual salary by Louis XV (1710-1774) to teach in all the provinces, she trained more than 4,000 pupils during her career. Du Coudray also established a veterinary (the medical treatment of animals) school in 1780.

Source: Uglow, Jennifer S., ed., *The Continuum Dictionary of Women's Biography*. New York: Continuum, 1989, p. 175.

c. 1790 ▪ **Marie La Chapelle** (1769-1821), a French obstetrician, organized a maternity and children's hospital at Port Royal in France. Training midwives (women who assist in the birthing process) from many European countries, La Chapelle introduced several innovations that helped save the lives of mothers and babies during childbirth. She also wrote an important three-volume work on obstetrics (the treatment of women during pregnancy and after childbirth) that became a major reference text for many years.

Source: Chicago, Judy, *The Dinner Party*. New York: Anchor, 1979, p. 191

1804 ▪ **Elizabeth Marshall** (1768-1836) was the first woman to work as a pharmacist in the United States. She operated the apothecary (a store for selling medicine) opened by her grandfather in Philadelphia, Pennsylvania, from 1804 to 1825. Marshall graduated in 1857 from the Women's Medical College of Pennsylvania, one of the only medical schools open to women at the time.

Source: Kane, Nathan Joseph, *Famous First Facts*. New York: Wilson, 1981, p. 459.

A Deadly Outbreak

A smallpox outbreak raged through eighteenth-century Europe, largely because of cramped living conditions and lack of sanitation (clean living conditions). One in ten persons died of the disease, many of them children and the elderly. It was believed that one in three persons in London had facial pit marks, or scarring, from smallpox.

1812 ▪ **Miranda Stuart** (1795-1865), an English physician, became the first female doctor in Britain when she received a medical degree from the University of Edinburgh in Scotland. In order to practice medicine she disguised herself as a man and took the name "James Berry." Starting as a military doctor, Stuart ended her career as Inspector General of British hospitals in Canada. Upon Stuart's death, an autopsy (an examination of a body after death) revealed that she was a woman; as a result, she was denied a funeral with military honors.

Source: Uglow, Jennifer S., ed., *The Continuum Dictionary of Women's Biography.* New York: Continuum, 1989, pp. 523-24.

c. 1820 ▪ **Marie Anne Victoire Boivin** (1773-1847), a French obstetrician (a doctor who specializes in the care of women and infants before, during, and after birth), invented a vaginal speculum (an instrument for inspecting or medicating the vagina). She was also one of the first obstetricians to listen to a fetal heartbeat with a stethoscope (an instrument used to hear the sounds of the body). Although Boivin did not receive recognition for her work in France, she was honored for her work in women's medicine in 1827 when she was awarded an honorary medical degree from the University of Marburg in Germany.

Source: Uglow, Jennifer S., ed., *The Continuum Dictionary of Women's Biography.* New York: Continuum, 1989, pp. 523-24.

1834 ▪ **Marie Durocher** (1809-1893), a French-Brazilian obstetrician (a doctor who specializes in the care of women and infants before, during, and after birth), received the first diploma granted by the Medical School of Rio de Janeiro. One of the first female doctors in Latin America, Durocher practiced medicine in Brazil for sixty years. She was greatly influenced by the teachings of French obstetrician Marie Boivin.

Source: Uglow, Jennifer S., ed., *The Continuum Dictionary of Women's Biography.* New York: Continuum, 1989, p. 179.

1835 ▪ **Harriot Kezia Hunt** (1805-1875), an American physician, is often considered the first woman to practice medicine in the United States. She opened an office with her sister Sarah, who left the practice when she got married in 1840. Harriot Hunt applied several times to Harvard Medical School, but was refused admission until she was accepted by Dean Oliver Wendall Holmes (1809-1894) in 1850. (She was forced to withdraw, however, when the male students rioted in protest.) In 1843 Hunt organized the Ladies' Physiological Society in Boston, Massachusetts, and in 1853 she was awarded an honorary medical degree from the Female Medical College of Pennsylvania.

Source: James, Edward T., and others, *Notable American Women, 1607-1950: A Biographical Dictionary.* Cambridge, Massachusetts: Harvard University Press, 1971, pp. 235-37.

1838 ▪ Mary Sargeant Neal Gove Nichols (1810-1884), an American feminist, was the first American woman to lecture on female anatomy (body structure), physiology (body functions), and hygiene (a term referring to preventive practices that contribute to good health). She began her career as a public speaker in Lynn and Boston, Massachusetts. Nichols also became a well-known novelist, as well as a writer in the field of health care.

Elizabeth Blackwell was the first woman to receive a medical degree in the United States.

Source: James, Edward T., and others, *Notable American Women, 1607-1950: A Biographical Dictionary.* Cambridge, Massachusetts: Harvard University Press, 1971, pp. 627-29.

1849 ▪ Elizabeth Blackwell (1821-1910), an English-born American doctor, became the first woman to receive a medical degree in the United States. She graduated from Geneva Medical College in Geneva, New York. With her sister Emily, Blackwell cofounded the New York Infirmary for Indigent (poor, without a source of income) Women and Children, the only hospital in the United States with an all-female staff. The sisters also started the Women's Medical College of New York,

which was attached to the infirmary. Blackwell was professor of hygiene (a term referring to preventive practices that contribute to good health) at the college until 1899, when female students were accepted at Cornell Medical School.

Source: Read, Phyllis J., and Bernard L. Witlieb, *The Book of Women's Firsts.* New York: Random House, 1992, pp. 54-55.

1851 ▪ Sarah Read Adamson Dolley (1829-1909), an American physician and feminist, was the first woman to serve as a hospital intern in the United States. After completing a one-year internship (supervised medical practice) at Blockley Hospital in Philadelphia, Pennsylvania, Adamson made her career in private practice in Rochester, New York.

Source: James, Edward T., and others, *Notable American Women, 1607-1950: A Biographical Dictionary.* Cambridge, Massachusetts: Harvard University Press, pp. 497-99.

Florence Nightingale, an English nurse and hospital administrator, introduced the system of modern nursing.

1854 ▪ Florence Nightingale (1820-1910), an English nurse and hospital administrator, introduced the system of modern nursing. While working as a volunteer nurse in the Crimean War (1854-1856), she was appalled by the filthy conditions in British military hospitals. As a result of Nightingale's use of clean medical supplies and facilities, the death rate among wounded soldiers declined from 42 percent to 2.2 percent. After returning from the war in 1856, she established the Nightingale School and Home for Nurses in England. Nightingale published *Notes on Nursing,* the first textbook for nurses, in 1906. In 1907 she was the first woman to receive the Order of Merit (an honor bestowed by the British monarchy).

Source: McGrayne, Sharon Bertsch, *Nobel Prize Women in Science: Their Lives, Struggles and Momentous Discoveries.* New York: Birch Lane Press, 1993, p. 252.

c. 1856 ▪ Emily Blackwell (1826-1910), an English-born American physician, was the first female doctor to have a large major surgery practice. She worked throughout her life with her sister, Elizabeth Blackwell (the first woman to earn a medical degree in the Unites States). For over forty years Emily helped manage the New York Infirmary, which she and Elizabeth founded in 1856. Emily Blackwell also was dean and professor of obstetrics (the care of women during pregnancy and after childbirth) and diseases of women at the Women's Medical College.

Source: James, Edward T., and others, *Notable American Women, 1607-1950: A Biographical Dictionary*. Cambridge, Massachusetts: Harvard University Press, 1971, pp. 165-67.

1858 ▪ **Marie Zakrzewska** (1829-1902), an American physician, introduced the practice of maintaining medical records. Zakrzewska helped Elizabeth and Emily Blackwell found the New York Infirmary for Indigent (poor, without a reliable source of income) Women and Children in 1856, then worked at the hospital for two years. During that time Zakrzewska became the first medical doctor to keep records of patients' treatment and progress.

Source: James, Edward T., and others, *Notable American Women, 1607-1950: A Biographical Dictionary*. Cambridge, Massachusetts: Harvard University Press, 1971, pp. 702-04.

1861 ▪ **Mary Edwards Walker** (1832-1919), an American surgeon, became the first woman to serve on the surgical staff of a modern army in wartime. Walker volunteered for service with the Union Army at the beginning of the American Civil War (1861-1865). When women were commissioned as doctors or nurses in 1864, Walker became acting assistant surgeon and a first lieutenant. An active supporter of women's rights, Walker dressed in male attire from the time of her Civil War service.

Source: Levin, Beatrice, *Women and Medicine: Pioneers Meeting the Challenge!* Lincoln, Nebraska: Media Publishing, 1988, p. 102.

1861 ▪ **Dorothea Lynde Dix** (1802-1887), an American nurse, developed the Army Nursing Corps. In 1861, at the outbreak of the Civil War (1861-1865), Dix was appointed chief of nurses for the Union Army. Turning public buildings into hospitals, she organized thousands of volunteer nurses into the Army Nursing Corps. Dix established rigid and somewhat idiosyncratic standards—she felt that her nurses should be Christian women of high moral character, over thirty years old, and "plain" in appearance. Dix served as head of the Corps until 1866.

Source: Read, Phyllis J., and Bernard L. Witlieb, *The Book of Women's Firsts.* New York: Random House, 1992, pp. 123-24.

1863 ▪ Mary Harris Thompson (1829-1895), an American physician and surgeon, was the first woman to perform major surgery. A specialist in abdominal and pelvic surgery, she developed an abdominal needle that was widely used at the time. For many years Thompson was the only woman performing surgery in the Midwest. She was also instrumental in the founding of the Woman's Hospital Medical College in Chicago, Illinois, in 1870 and served as the college's first professor of hygiene from 1870 until 1877.

Source: James, Edward T., and others, *Notable American Women, 1607-1950: A Biographical Dictionary.* Cambridge, Massachusetts: Harvard University Press, 1971, pp. 454-55.

1864 ▪ Emeline Roberts Jones, an American dentist, was the first woman to practice dentistry independently. In 1855 she began her career in Danielsonville, Connecticut, as an assistant to her husband. After training with her husband for four years, Jones became his partner. Upon her husband's death in 1864, Jones took over the couple's practice.

Source: McCullough, Joan, *First of All: Significant "Firsts" by American Women.* New York: Holt, 1980, p. 116.

c. 1865 ▪ Rebecca Lee (1833-?), an American physician, was the first black female to practice medicine in the United States. Lee earned her degree from the New England Female Medical College in Boston, Massachusetts, in 1864. After the Civil War (1861-1865) ended, she established a practice in Richmond, Virginia.

Source: Levin, Beatrice, *Women and Medicine: Pioneers Meeting the Challenge!* Lincoln, Nebraska: Media Publishing, 1988, p. 96.

c. 1865 ▪ **Elizabeth Garrett Anderson** (1836-1917) was the first English female physician. After being refused admission to various medical schools, she studied at the London Hospital and at St. Andrew's. Anderson had to dissect (cut apart for study) cadavers (dead bodies used for medical experiments and research) in her own home because, as a woman, she was not allowed to work in dissecting rooms. After receiving her medical degree in 1865, Anderson became a pioneer for other women in the profession and established the New Hospital for Women and Children. From 1873 until 1892, Anderson was the first and only female member of the British Medical Association. In 1908 she was elected mayor of Aldeburgh, becoming the first female mayor in England.

Source: Ogilvie, Marilyn Bailey, *Women in Science: Antiquity through the Nineteenth Century.* Cambridge, Massachusetts: M.I.T. Press, 1986, p. 21.

1870 ▪ **Clara A. Swain** (1834-1910), an American physician, was the first woman to represent the United States as a trained medical missionary in Asia. Appointed by the Woman's Foreign Missionary Society of the Methodist Episcopal Church, she joined the mission of Bareilly, India, in 1870. Four years later, Swain opened the first hospital for women in India. She dedicated her life to the mission, greatly expanding its medical facilities. The Clara Swain Hospital still stands at Bareilly and serves a large number of women and men each year.

Source: James, Edward T., and others, *Notable American Women, 1607-1950: A Biographical Dictionary.* Cambridge, Massachusetts: Harvard University Press, 1971, pp. 411-13.

1872 ▪ **Mary Jane Safford** (1834-1891), an American physician, was the first woman to perform an ovariotomy (the surgical cutting of an ovary). Safford performed the surgery while studying at the University of Breslau in Germany.

Source: James, Edward T., and others, *Notable American Women, 1607-1950: A Biographical Dictionary.* Cambridge, Massachusetts: Harvard University Press, 1971, pp. 220-22.

1886 ▪ **Linda A. J. Richards** (1841-1930), a pioneering American nurse and educator, founded a training school for nurses at Doshisha Hospital in Kyoto, Japan. Richards was also the first person to receive an American diploma in nursing. In 1962 the National League for Nursing created an award in Richards's name. The award was to be given periodically to a practicing nurse who made a pioneering contribution to the nursing field.

Source: James, Edward T., and others, *Notable American Women, 1607-1950: A Biographical Dictionary.* Cambridge, Massachusetts: Harvard University Press, 1971, pp. 148-50.

1875 ▪ **Jennie Kidd Trout** (1841-?) became the first licensed female doctor in Canada when she graduated from the Women's Medical College of Pennsylvania. During her career Trout helped to establish two women's medical colleges, worked to gain the admission of women to medical schools, and became a fervent promoter of women in medicine. In 1883 Trout helped to endow (provide money for) the Women's Medical College of Kingston. She was one of the most significant contributors to breaking down the barriers that prevented women from entering medicine in Canada.

Source: Dembski, "Jennie Kidd Trout and the Founding of the Women's Medical Colleges at Kingston and Toronto," *Ontario History.* Volume 3, number 77, 1985.

1882 ▪ **Aletta Jacobs** (1849-1929), a Dutch physician, started the world's first birth control clinic, in Amsterdam, the Netherlands. Despite opposition from the medical establishment, Jacobs operated the clinic for 30 years.

Source: Uglow, Jennifer S., ed., *The Continuum Dictionary of Women's Biography.* New York: Continuum, 1989, p. 279.

1877 ▪ **Anna Tomaszewicz-Dobrska** (1854-1918), a Polish physician, was the second woman in her country to become a doctor and the first to return to Poland to practice medicine. After studying medicine in Switzerland, Austria, Germany, and Russia, Tomaszewicz-Dobrska established a practice in Warsaw, Poland, in 1877. Five years later she became the first woman to serve as chief of Lying-In Hospital No. 2 in Warsaw. She held the post until the hospital closed in 1911.

Source: Uglow, Jennifer S., ed., *The Continuum Dictionary of Women's Biography.* New York: Continuum, 1989, p. 542.

1878 ▪ Sophia Jex-Blake (1840-1912), an English doctor, became the first female physician in Scotland. Although she and five other women fought successfully to be admitted to the University of Edinburgh in 1869, university officials reversed their decision in 1873. Jex-Blake eventually earned her medical degree from the University of Bern, Germany, in 1877, then went to Scotland to practice medicine. An assertive advocate of women's rights, Jex-Blake founded the London School of Medicine for Women in 1874 and the Women's Hospital in Edinburgh in 1885. She organized the Edinburgh School of Medicine for women in 1894.

Source: Ogilvie, Marilyn Bailey, *Women in Science: Antiquity through the Nineteenth Century.* Cambridge, Massachusetts: M.I.T. Press, p. 105-07.

Clara Barton, an American nurse, was the founder and first president of the American Red Cross.

c. 1880s ▪ Constance Stone (1856-1902), a Canadian doctor, was the first woman to practice medicine in Victoria, Australia. After earning her medical credentials at the Women's Medical College in Philadelphia, Pennsylvania, she returned to Australia to set up private practice. Stone was later instrumental in the establishment of the Queen Victoria Hospital for the indigent (poor) people of Melbourne, Australia.

Source: Uglow, Jennifer S., *The Continuum Dictionary of Women's Biography.* New York: Continuum, 1989, p. 519.

1881 ▪ Clara Barton (1821-1912), an American nurse, was the founder and first president of the **American Red Cross**, an organization she headed until 1904. Barton modeled the American Red Cross on the International Committee of the Red

Cross, which was formed in Geneva, Switzerland, in 1863. Among the disasters the Red Cross responded to under Barton's leadership were catastrophic fires in Michigan, an earthquake in Charleston, South Carolina, and floods on the Ohio and Mississippi Rivers.

Source: Read, Phyllis J., and Bernard L. Witlieb, *The Book of Women's Firsts.* New York: Random House, 1992, pp. 40-41.

1883 ▪ **Edith Pechey-Phipson** (1845-1908), a pioneering English physician, became the first woman to direct the Cama Hospital in Bombay, India. She was also the founder of the Pechey-Phipson Sanitarium near Nasik, India.

Source: Uglow, Jennifer S., *The Continuum Dictionary of Women's Biography.* New York: Continuum, 1989, p. 427.

1883 ▪ **Susan Hayhurst** became the first female pharmacist in the United States after receiving her degree from the Philadelphia College of Pharmacy. She graduated in 1857 from the Women's Medical College of Pennsylvania, one of the only schools founded for women.

Source: McCullough, Joan, *First of All: Significant "Firsts" by American Women.* New York: Holt, 1980, p. 119.

1889 ▪ **Susan La Flesche Piccotte** (1865-1915) was the first Native-American woman to study Western medicine. The daughter of an Omaha chief, she received her degree from the Women's Medical College of Pennsylvania in 1889. Piccotte then returned to practice medicine among her people, founding a hospital in 1913.

Source: James, Edward T., and others, *Notable American Women, 1607-1950: A Biographical Dictionary.* Cambridge, Massachusetts: Harvard University Press, 1971, pp. 65- 66.

1890s ▪ **Mary Kalopathakes,** a Greek physician, is credited with being the first person to establish nursing as a profession in Greece. She earned her medical degree in Paris, France, in the 1880s.

Source: Levin, Beatrice, *Women and Medicine: Pioneers Meeting the Challenge!* Lincoln, Nebraska: Media Publishing, 1988, p. 78.

1895 ▪ **Lilian Murray** (1871-1959), an English dentist, was the first woman licensed to practice dentistry in Britain. Although she served three years of apprenticeship, she was not allowed to enter the National Dental Hospital in London to practice her profession. Murray then moved to Edinburgh, Scotland, where she was licensed at Edinburgh Dental Hospital in 1895. Murray married her teacher, Robert Lindsay, who was also a dentist. The couple established a joint dental practice in Edinburgh.

Source: Uglow, Jennifer S., ed., *The Continuum Dictionary of Women's Biography.* New York: Continuum, 1989, p. 393.

1896 ▪ **Ada Stewart** became the first industrial nurse when she was hired by the Vermont Marble Company of Proctor, Vermont.

Source: Kane, Nathan Joseph, *Famous First Facts.* New York: Wilson, 1981, p. 468.

1898 ▪ **Maude Elizabeth Seymour Abbott** (1869-1940), a Canadian physician, was the first person to develop a medical catalogue of the human circulatory system (blood vessels, veins, etc.). In 1898, while working as curator (superintendent) of the medical museum at McGill University in Montreal, Canada, Abbott published the *Osler Catalogue of the Circulatory System.*

Source: Uglow, Jennifer S., ed., *The Continuum Dictionary of Women's Biography.* New York: Continuum, 1989, p. 2.

1898 ▪ **Elizabeth Hurdon** (1868-1941), a Canadian-born gynecologist (a doctor who treats the female reproductive system) and pathologist (a doctor who studies the structure of disease), became the first woman to serve on the staff of the Johns Hopkins Hospital in Baltimore, Maryland. Hurdon simultaneously held a faculty appointment in the Johns Hopkins University Medical School in Baltimore, Maryland.

Source: James, Edward T., and others, *Notable American Women, 1607-1950: A Biographical Dictionary.* Cambridge, Massachusetts: Harvard University Press, 1971, pp. 242-44.

Pelletier Joined Hospital Staff

Madeleine (Anne) Pelletier (1874-1939), a French physician, was the first woman appointed to the staff of the Assistance Publique (Public Assistance) in Paris, France. In 1906 Pelletier became the first woman in France to qualify to work in mental hospitals.

1898 ▪ Dorothy Reed (1874-1964) and **Margaret Long,** American physicians, were the first women to perform medical duties in a U.S. Navy hospital. As medical students, Reed and Long worked in the operating room and the bacteriological laboratories at the Brooklyn Navy Yard Hospital, New York City, in 1898.

Source: Read, Phyllis J., and Bernard L. Witlieb, *The Book of Women's Firsts.* New York: Random House, 1992, pp. 362-63.

1899 ▪ Ethel Gordon Fenwick (1857-1947), an English nurse, organized the International Council of Nurses. The Council was the first such organization for health care professionals, as well as the first for professional women. Fenwick served as the first president. A decade earlier she had helped to organize the British Nurses' Association and served as its first president. Working throughout her life for higher standards in the nursing profession, Fenwick started the Matrons' Council of Great Britain and Ireland in 1894 and went on to found the British College of Nurses in 1926.

Source: Uglow, Jennifer S., ed., *The Continuum Dictionary of Women's Biography.* New York: Continuum, 1989, p. 200.

c. 1900 ▪ Trinidad Tescon (1848-1928), a Filipina nurse and freedom fighter, introduced Red Cross assistance in the Philippines. During the Philippine Revolution (a movement to gain independence from Spanish rule), Tescon organized women as nurses and set up a makeshift hospital also staffed by Red Cross volunteers. Known as "Mother of Baik-Na-Bota," she extended the work of the Red Cross throughout the Philippines after the revolution. She organized a nursing facility and founded a hospital in the fort of Baik-na-Bota. Tescon's work was recognized by the International Red Cross.

Source: Uglow, Jennifer, ed., *The Continuum Dictionary of Women's Biography.* New York, Continuum, 1989, p. 536.

c. 1900 ▪ Mary Ann Scharlieb (1845-1930), an English physician specializing in abdominal surgery, was the founder of the Victoria Hospital for Caste and Gosha Women, in Madras, India. Alternating her professional life between Britain and India, Scharlieb helped to form a women's medical service in India during World War I (1914-1918). In 1920 she became one of the first female magistrates (judges) in England.

Source: Uglow, Jennifer S., ed., *The Continuum Dictionary of Women's Biography*. New York: Continuum, 1989, p. 481.

1900 ▪ **Sister Mary Alphonsa** (1851-1926) cofounded, with **Alice Huber,** the nation's first hospice. (An alternative to standard hospitalization, hospices are places that deal specifically with the emotional and physical needs of terminal, or fatally ill, patients.) The two women opened their hospice in New York City to care for people suffering from incurable cancer. The daughter of writer Nathanial Hawthorne (1804-1864) and Sophia Peabody, Alphonsa converted to Roman Catholicism in 1891, after her husband's death. She then joined the lay sisters (women who have not been consecrated as nuns) of the Dominican third order.

Source: Read, Phyllis J., and Bernard L. Witlieb, *The Book of Women's Firsts*. New York: Random House, 1992, pp. 248-49.

1900 ▪ **Sophia Palmer** (1853-1920), an American nurse, became the first editor in chief of the *American Journal of Nursing*. Palmer was active throughout her life in nursing and nursing administration.

Source: James, Edward T., and others, *Notable American Women, 1607-1950: A Biographical Dictionary*. Cambridge, Massachusetts: Harvard University Press, 1971, pp. 14- 15.

1901 ▪ **Anita Newcomb McGee** (1864-1940), an American physician, drafted the section of the Army Reorganization Act of 1901 that established the Army Nurse Corps. McGee was opposed, however, by the American Red Cross, which regarded the recruitment and deployment of nurses as its primary function. McGee was prevented from serving as director of the Army Nurse Corps by legislation that required the director to be a graduate nurse.

Source: James, Edward T., and others, eds., *Notable American Women, 1607-1950: A Biographical Dictionary*. Cambridge, Massachusetts: Harvard University Press, 1971, pp. 464-66.

c. 1902 ▪ **Sheldon Amos Elgood,** an English doctor, was the first female physician appointed by the Egyptian government. Having received her medical degree from London University in 1900, Elgood opened the first outpatient department for women and children in an Egyptian government hospital. She also founded the first free children's dispensaries (pharmacies) in Egypt.

Source: Levin, Beatrice, *Women and Medicine: Pioneers Meeting the Challenge!* Lincoln, Nebraska: Media Publishing, 1988, p. 67.

1903 ▪ **Emily Dunning** (1876-1961), an American physician, was the first female ambulance surgeon. She achieved this distinction when, as a staff surgeon at Gouverneur Hospital in New York City, she answered her first emergency call in a horse-drawn vehicle on June 29, 1903.

Source: Read, Phyllis J., and Bernard L. Witlieb, *The Book of Women's Firsts.* New York: Random House, 1992, pp. 128-29.

1908 ▪ **Sara Josephine Baker** (1873-1945), an American physician, was the founder of the Bureau of Child Hygiene in New York City. Baker worked on behalf of public health issues throughout her life. When she refused a lectureship at New York University because women could not be admitted to graduate programs, the university changed its policy. In 1917 Baker then became the first woman to earn a doctorate of public health, from New York University Bellevue Hospital Medical School.

Source: James, Edward T., and others, eds., *Notable American Women, 1607-1950: A Biographical Dictionary.* Cambridge, Massachusetts: Harvard University Press, 1971, pp. 85- 86.

1910 ▪ **Elinor McGrath,** an American veterinarian, became the first female veterinarian (a doctor who specializes in animal care) when she graduated from the Chicago Veterinary College. McGrath practiced in Chicago, Illinois, for 37 years before moving to Hot Springs, Arkansas, in 1947 to treat alligators and ostriches.

Source: McCullough, Joan, *First of All: Significant "Firsts" by American Women.* New York: Holt, 1980, p. 112.

1911 ▪ **Clara Dutton Noyes** (1869-1936), an American nurse, founded the first school for midwives in the United States at Bellevue Hospital in New York City. (A midwife assists in the birth of babies.) Noyes devoted her life to the nursing profession and was active in nursing administration in several organizations throughout her life.

Source: Read, Phyllis J., and Bernard L. Witlieb, *The Book of Women's Firsts*. New York: Random House, 1992, pp. 318-19.

1913 ▪ **Carolyn C. Van Blarcom** (1879-1960), an American nurse, was the first female nurse in America to become a licensed midwife (a person who assists in the birth of babies). She earned her license in England because the United States did not formally train or license midwives at the time.

Source: Read, Phyllis J., and Bernard L. Witlieb, *The Book of Women's Firsts*. New York: Random House, 1992, p. 460.

Bertha Van Hoosen was the cofounder and first president of the American Medical Women's Association.

1914 ▪ **Elsie Inglis** (1874-1917), a British doctor and feminist, founded the Scottish Women's Hospitals. Organized to help in the war effort during World War I (1914-1918), Inglis's group consisted of an entirely female staff. The women operated two medical units in France and one in Serbia (headed by Inglis herself). A lifelong advocate of women's rights, Inglis cofounded, with Jessie MacGregor, the only maternity center run by women in Scotland. The institution later became the Elsie Inglis Hospital.

Source: Uglow, Jennifer S., ed., *The Continuum Dictionary of Women's Biography*. New York: Continuum, 1989, pp. 273-74.

1915 ▪ **Bertha Van Hoosen** (1863-1952), an American physician, was the cofounder and first president of the American Medical Women's Association. Trained in gynecology (the treatment and care of the female reproductive system), obstetrics (medical treatment dealing with matters of childbirth), and surgery, Van Hoosen practiced medicine in Chicago, Illinois, and in 1918 was appointed professor and head of obstetrics at Loyola University Medical School.

Source: Read, Phyllis J., and Bernard L. Witlieb, *The Book of Women's Firsts.* New York: Random House, 1992, pp. 463-64.

1916 ▪ Margaret Sanger (1883-1966), an American birth control advocate, opened the first birth-control clinic in the United States with her sister, Ethyl Byrne. Located in Brownsville, a neighborhood of Brooklyn, New York, the clinic provided information about birth control to poverty-stricken women. Police soon shut the facility down because "obscene materials" (contraceptives) were being dispensed; as a result, Sanger spent a year in jail.

Although Sanger's promotion of birth control brought her indictments and arrests, public and court support for her work gradually grew. In 1923 Sanger organized the first American conference on birth control and formed a committee to lobby for birth-control laws, which helped establish clinics around the world. In 1925 Sanger organized an international birth-control conference. By 1930, 55 clinics had been opened across the country. Sanger devoted her life to educating women about birth control, and in 1953 she was the founder and first president of the International Planned Parenthood Federation.

Source: Read, Phyllis J., and Bernard L. Witlieb, *The Book of Women's Firsts.* New York: Random House, 1992, pp. 391-93.

1921 ▪ Marie Charlotte Carmichael Stopes (c. 1880-1958), a British birth-control advocate, founded the first family planning center in England, at Islington. Stopes devoted her life to the cause of birth control, and was the designer of a pessary (a device worn in the vagina), which she called the "pro-race" cap. A brilliant scholar, Stopes also held a doctorate and was the first woman to join the science faculty at the University of Manchester in 1904.

Source: Uglow, Jennifer, ed., *The Continuum Dictionary of Women's Biography.* New York, Continuum, 1989, p. 520.

Margaret Sanger was the founder and first president of the International Planned Parenthood Federation.

1925 ▪ **Cecily Williams** (1893-?), an English physician, was the first female doctor assigned overseas by the British Colonial Office. Williams went to work in Koforidua, Ghana, where she was the first person to identify the childhood nutritional disease "kwashiorkor," one of the most widespread pediatric (childhood) diseases of the tropics. She later worked in Malaya, where she was appointed head the division of Maternity and Child Welfare, attaining the highest position held by a woman until that time in the Colonial Service.

Source: Levin, Beatrice, *Women and Medicine: Pioneers Meeting the Challenge!* Lincoln, Nebraska: Media Publishing, 1988, pp. 582-83.

1926 ▪ **Amelia Villa** (?-1942) was the first female physician in Bolivia. After earning a medical degree in 1926, Villa worked in pediatrics (the treatment of children's diseases) for the rest of her life. At the end of her career Villa was honored by the Bolivian government, which also named a children's ward for her at the hospital in Oruro.

Source: Chicago, Judy, *The Dinner Party.* New York: Anchor, 1979, p. 19.

1928 ▪ **Mary Breckinridge** (1881-1965), an American nurse, founded the Frontier Nursing Service to provide medical services to isolated mountain families in the United States. Emphasizing care for mothers and children, the organization evolved into the American Association of Nurse-Midwives.

Source: Read, Phyllis J., and Bernard L. Witlieb, *The Book of Women's Firsts.* New York: Random House, 1992, p. 65.

1929 ▪ **Adah B. Samuels Thoms** (1863-1943), a pioneering African-American nurse, published *Pathfinders: A History of the Progress of Colored Graduate Nurses.* Thoms was the first person to receive the Mary Mahoney Medal from the National Association of Colored Graduate Nurses. She was recognized for her distinguished contributions to nursing.

Source: James, Edward T., and others, eds., *Notable American Women, 1607-1950: A Biographical Dictionary.* Cambridge, Massachusetts: Harvard University Press, 1971, pp. 455-57.

c. 1930 ▪ **Alice Isabel Bever Bryan** (1902-1992), an American psychologist, was the first person to develop the concept of bibliotherapy. (This therapy technique involves the reading of books to promote mental health.) Bryan's theory was used as a preventive measure for healthy people, as well as a therapy for the mentally ill. She worked as a psychologist at Columbia University in New York City.

Source: Bailey, Brooke, *The Remarkable Lives of 100 Women Healers and Scientists.* Holbrook, Massachusetts: Bob Adams, 1994, pp. 32-33.

1930 ▪ **Ellen Church** (1905-), an American nurse, became the first woman to serve as an airline stewardess. A registered nurse, Church suggested the name and idea of this new profession to her superiors at Boeing Air Transport. On May 15, 1930, on a flight between Cheyenne, Wyoming, and Oakland, California, she became the first person to serve in this capacity. Church set a precedent, and for the next 12 years all stewardesses were required to be registered nurses.

1930 ▪ **Martha Wollstein** (1868-1939), an American physician, became the first female member of the American Pediatric Society. She was honored in 1930 for her extensive research on meningitis (a swelling of the membranes around the brain and spinal cord), mumps, pneumonia, and polio (an inflammatory viral infection of the spinal cord that can lead to paralysis).

Source: James, Edward T., and others, *Notable American Women, 1607-1950: A Biographical Dictionary.* Cambridge, Massachusetts: Harvard University Press, 1971, pp. 642-44.

1933 ▪ **Christine Murrell** (1874-1933) was the first woman elected as a member of the General Medical Council of Great Britain, in London in 1933. Murrell had a career as a physician in general practice, serving in the Women's Emergency Corps during World War I (1914-1918) and publishing a book, *Women and Health,* in 1923.

Source: Uglow, Jennifer S., ed., *The Continuum Dictionary of Women's Biography.* New York: Continuum, 1989, pp. 393-94.

1933 ▪ **Elizabeth Kenny (Sister Kenny)** (1880-1952), an Australian nurse, founded a clinic for the treatment of poliomyelitis (also known as "polio"; a viral inflammation, or swelling, of the spinal cord that often results in muscle paraly-

sis). Kenny introduced a new therapy technique, which emphasized muscle exercises over immobilization (the restriction of movement) of the legs with casts and splints. She went on to found clinics in Minneapolis, Minnesota (1920), and Britain (1937).

Source: Magnusson, Magnus *Larousse Biographical Dictionary.* Edinburgh: Larousse Kingfisher Chambers, Inc., 1994, p. 820.

1936 ▪ **Alice Hamilton** (1869-1970), an American physician, was the founder of industrial medical studies. In her work, Hamilton identified the sources of toxic (or poisonous) substances in factories and mines that had an effect on human health. Hamilton received a medical degree from the University of Michigan Medical School at Ann Arbor in 1893.

Source: Vare, Ethelie Ann, and Greg Ptacek, *Mothers of Invention: From the Bra to the Bomb, Forgotten Women and Their Unforgettable Ideas.* New York: William Morrow, 1988, p. 117.

American physician Alice Hamilton was one of the first researchers in the field of industrial medical studies.

1938 ▪ **Kate Campbell Hurd-Mead** (1867-1941), an American physician, published *A History of Women in Medicine from the Earliest Times to the Beginning of the Nineteenth Century,* the first comprehensive chronicle of women in medicine. A specialist in women's and children's diseases, Hurd-Mead also established a nurses' organization, the Baltimore Dispensary for Working Women and Girls, and the Medical Women's International Association.

Source: Chicago, Judy, *The Dinner Party.* New York: Anchor, 1979, p. 191.

c. 1952 ▪ **Virginia Apgar** (1909-1974), an American physician, invented a standard newborn health evaluation system, known as the "Apgar Score," for calculating the general health of infants in the first moments after birth. (The Apgar Score measures five components—healthy skin tone, breathing, pulse, muscle tone, and response to stimulation—on an "acceptable standard rating" point scale.) Apgar was also the first person to become a full professor of anesthesiology (a branch of medicine specializing in the use of anesthesia, or drugs that render patients unconscious for surgery). Apgar attained this rank at Columbia University in New York City as a result of her achievements in neonatal (newborn infant) care.

Source: Vare, Ethelie Ann, and Greg Ptacek, *Mothers of Invention: From the Bra to the Bomb, Forgotten Women and Their Unforgettable Ideas.* New York: William Morrow, 1988, pp. 133- 34.

1955 ▪ Emma Sadler Moss (1898-1970), an American physician, became the first woman president of a major medical society. She was elected head of the American Society of Clinical Pathologists at the organization's 34th annual meeting in 1955. Moss practiced medicine at Charity Hospital in New Orleans, Louisiana.

Source: Read, Phyllis J., and Bernard L. Witlieb, *The Book of Women's Firsts.* New York: Random House, 1992, p. 300.

Logan Performed Surgery

Myra Adele Logan (1908-1977), an African-American surgeon, was the first woman to perform open heart surgery. Logan graduated from Atlanta University in Georgia in 1927 and earned a master's degree in psychology from Columbia University. In addition to her surgical practice, she conducted research on the then-new antibiotic drugs, such as Aureomycin. In the 1960s Logan began studying breast cancer, developing a slower X-ray process that could more accurately detect differences in the density of tissue and thus help discover tumors much earlier. She was also the first African-American woman elected a fellow of the American College of Surgeons.

1958 ▪ Marion E. Kenworthy (1891-1980) was the first female president of the American Psychoanalytic Association. Kenworthy had a distinguished career in psychiatry. She was the first director of the mental hygiene clinic of the Young Women's Christian Association (YWCA) and the first female professor of psychiatry at Columbia University in New York City (1930).

Source: Read, Phyllis J., and Bernard L. Witlieb, *The Book of Women's Firsts.* New York: Random House, 1992, pp. 240-41.

1961 ▪ Janet Graeme Travell (1901-) was the first woman to serve as the personal physician for a United States president. She was the official doctor for President John F. Kennedy (served in office from 1961-1963) and remained in the position of White House Physician until 1965.

Janet Graeme Travell was the personal physician for President John F. Kennedy.

Source: Read, Phyllis J., and Bernard L. Witlieb, *The Book of Women's Firsts.* New York: Random House, 1992, pp. 447-48.

1966 ▪ Elizabeth "Bess" Wallace Truman (1885-1982) was the first woman to receive a Medicare identification card. The wife of former President Harry S Truman (1884-1972; served in office 1945-1953), she was presented her card (No. 2) by President Lyndon Baines Johnson at the Truman Library in Independence, Missouri. Medicare was created by Public Law 89-97 on July 30, 1965, as a national health insurance plan in the United States,

Source: Kane, Nathan Joseph, *Famous First Facts.* New York: Wilson, 1981, p. 385.

1975 ▪ May Edward Chinn (1896-1980), an African-American physician, was the cofounder of the Susan Smith McKinney Stewart Society in New York City. This organization was designed to promote the role of African-American women in medicine. Chinn was also the first African-American woman to graduate from the University of Bellevue Medical Center and the first African-American woman to intern at Harlem Hospital, both in 1926.

Source: Bailey, Brooke, *The Remarkable Lives of 100 Women Healers and Scientists.* Holbrook, Massachusetts: Bob Adams, 1994, pp. 44-45.

1975 ▪ Mamphela Ramphele (1948-), a South African physician and political activist, was the founder of the Zanempilo Health Clinic at King William's Town in 1975. She also founded the Ithuseng Community Health Centre in 1978. Working as an itinerant doctor, Ramphele was a friend of Mapetla Mohapi and journalist Steven Biko, both of whom died as a result of their protests against apartheid (racial segregation).

Source: Uglow, Jennifer S., ed., *The Continuum Dictionary of Women's Biography.* New York: Continuum, 1989, p. 447.

1979 ▪ Josephine Mary Taylor Barnes (1912-), a British obstetrician and gynecologist, became the first female president of the British Medical Association. She worked on behalf of women and women's medicine through out her life.

Source: Uglow, Jennifer S., ed., *The Continuum Dictionary of Women's Biography.* New York: Continuum, 1989, p. 49.

1990 ▪ Lori Cupp, a Native-American physician, became the first female Navaho Indian to become a surgeon. She graduated from Stanford University Medical School in 1990. She believed that Navaho culture, which is matriarchal (headed by women), was an asset in her medical specialty. Only 6 percent of surgeons were women in 1990.

Source: "Old Ways and New, in Harmony," *The New York Times.* February 17, 1994.

Military

1779 ▪ Margaret "Molly" Corbin (1751-1801) was the first female soldier in the Revolutionary War (1775-1783) and the first woman to receive a U.S. army pension. In 1776 Corbin accompanied her husband John, a cannoneer, in the battle at Fort Washington, New York. When John Corbin was killed in a British attack, Molly took his place. Reloading and firing his cannon until the battle was over, Corbin herself was disabled by a wound in the arm. In July 1779 she was awarded a full military pension by the Supreme Council of Pennsylvania. The Continental Congress additionally decided she was entitled to half of a soldier's disability pay for life. Corbin subsequently enlisted in the Invalid Regiment, a unit for wounded veterans. A monument was erected in Corbin's honor in 1916 at the United States Military Academy in West Point, New York.

Source: James, Edward T., and others, *Notable American Women, 1607-1950: A Biographical Dictionary,* Cambridge, Massachusetts: Harvard University Press, 1971, p. 386.

Physician May Edward Chinn cofounded the Susan Smith McKinney Stewart Society, an organization designed to promote the role of African-American women in medicine.

Margaret "Molly" Corbin was the first female soldier in the Revolutionary War. She took her husband's place in battle after he was killed during a British attack.

1802 ▪ **Deborah Sampson** (1760-1827), an American Revolutionary War (1775-1783) soldier, was the first woman on record to enlist in the U.S. Army. In 1782 Sampson enlisted as a man in the Fourth Massachusetts Regiment, adopting the name "Robert Shurtleff." When Sampson was hospitalized with a fever the following year, her true gender (or sex) was discovered and she was discharged from the army. In 1802, Sampson lectured on her military experience, becoming the first woman to do so.

Source: Chicago, Judy, *The Dinner Party.* New York: Anchor, 1979, p. 168.

c. 1820 ▪ **Augustina Zaragoza** (1786-1857; also known as Agostina La Saragossa) was the first female hero painted by Spanish artist Goya (1746-1828; full name, Goya y Lucientes). Zaragoza helped defend Saragossa, Spain, against French invaders in 1808. The "Maid of Saragossa" was later buried with full military honors.

Source: Williams, S. W., *Queenly Women, Crowned and Uncrowned.* New York: Marshall Cavendish, 1993, pp. 359-66.

1863 ▪ **Susan "Susie" Baker King Taylor** (1848-1912) was the first African-American woman to serve as a nurse in the U.S. armed services. In 1863, during the Civil War (1861-1865), Taylor nursed with the First Regiment of the South Carolina Volunteers.

Source: Smith, Jessie Carney, *Notable Black American Women.* Detroit: Gale Research, 1992, pp. 1108-13.

1865 ▪ **Mary Edwards Walker** (1832-1919), an American physician, was the first woman awarded the Congressional Medal of Honor. She was honored for her work as a surgeon during the Civil War (1861-1865).

Source: Parry, Melanie, ed., *Larousse Dictionary of Women.* New York: Larousse Kingfisher Chambers, Inc, 1995, p. 673.

1897 ▪ **Sarah Emma Edmonds** (1841-1898), a Canadian-born U.S. soldier, became the first and only female member of the Grand Army of the Republic (GAR), an organization of Civil War veterans. Enlisting in the Union Army sometime between in 1859 and 1861, Edmonds assumed a male identity under the name of "Franklin Thompson." She is considered the only woman to have served as a soldier in the U.S. Civil War (1861-1865), although other women were involved on both sides of the conflict in supporting positions. According to one source, Edmonds deserted the Army in 1863, then returned as a female nurse with the U.S. Christian Commission. In Edmonds she published her memoirs, *Nurse and Spy in the Union Army.*

Source: Read, Phyllis J., and Bernard L. Witlieb, *The Book of Women's Firsts.* New York: Random House, 1992, pp. 138-39.

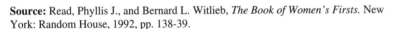

1917 ▪ **Mariya Bochkareva** (1889-19?), a Russian soldier, organized the "Women's Battalion of Death." After enlisting in the army at the beginning of World War I (1914-1918), Bochkavera became famous for her valor in battle. She received numerous medals for rescuing wounded soldiers from machine-gun fire on the front lines. By 1917 Russian troops were almost completely demoralized as they suffered defeat after defeat at the hands of the German and Austrian armies. During a trip to St. Petersburg that year, Bochkareva decided to improve morale by forming "The Women's Battalion of Death." Taking the name "Yashka," she organized nearly two thousand women volunteers into two battalions. The women marched into battle in July of 1917, but suffered extensive casualties. After the Russian Revolution (the Communist overthrow of the imperial government in 1917), Bochkareva was

Deborah Sampson, an American Revolutionary War soldier, was the first woman on record to enlist in the U.S. Army.

Augustina Zaragoza was the first female hero painted by Spanish artist Goya.

sentenced to death by the new government. She fled to the United States.

Source: Uglow, Jennifer S., ed., *The Continuum Dictionary of Women's Biography.* New York: Continuum, 1989, p. 74.

1918 ▪ Larissa Mikhailovna Reisner

(1895-1926), a Russian revolutionary and journalist, was the first woman to serve as a political commissar (Communist party official) in the Red Army. At the end of World War I (1914-1918) Reisner was a soldier and intelligence officer on the Eastern Front. In 1921 she became the first female Soviet ambassador (representative) to Afghanistan. Reisner's journalism and autobiographical writing appeared in several books before her early death from typhus (a bacterial disease).

Source: Uglow, Jennifer S., ed., *The Continuum Dictionary of Women's Biography.* New York: Continuum, 1989, p. 453.

1942 ▪ Ann Leah Fox (1918-), a Canadian nurse, was the first woman awarded the Purple Heart medal. Fox was wounded while serving as a military nurse at Pearl Harbor in Hawaii during the Japanese attack on December 7, 1941.

Source: Read, Phyllis J., and Bernard L. Witlieb, *The Book of Women's Firsts.* New York: Random House, 1992, p. 164.

1942 ▪ Mildred Helen McAfee (1900-), an American naval officer, became the first director of the newly formed Women Accepted for Volunteer Emergency Service (WAVES), a naval reserve program for women. At the time of her appointment in 1942, McAfee had been president of Wellesley College since 1936. Taking a leave of absence to head the WAVES, she returned to Wellesley after World War II (1939-1945).

Source: Kane, Nathan Joseph, *Famous First Facts.* New York: Wilson, 1981, p. 421.

1944 ▪ Cordelia E. Cook, an American army nurse, was the first woman awarded the Bronze Star. Cook received this honor in recognition for her work at an Italian field hospital during World War II (1939-1945) in the winter of 1943-1944. Although her area was repeatedly under attack and she herself was wounded, Cook continued to perform her duties. She was also awarded the Order of the Purple Heart for performing service while wounded, thus becoming the first woman who served during World War II to receive two military decorations.

Source: Read, Phyllis J., and Bernard L. Witlieb, *The Book of Women's Firsts.* New York: Random House, 1992, p. 101.

1947 ▪ Florence Aby Blanchfield (1882-1971), an American military officer, was the first woman to receive a regular commission in the United States Army when she was appointed lieutenant colonel. Blanchfield established her career in the Army Nurse Corps, joining in 1917 and achieving the rank of superintendent in 1943. With the passage of the Army-Navy Nurse Act in 1947, nurses were granted full status and Blanchfield finally received her commission.

Source: Bailey, Brooke, *The Remarkable Lives of 100 Women Healers and Scientists.* Holbrook, Massachusetts: Bob Adams, 1994, pp. 20-21.

1948 ▪ Frances L. Willoughby (1906-1984), an American physician, was the first female medical doctor to hold a regular U.S. Navy commission. During World War II (1939-1945), Willoughby had served in the naval reserve. In 1948 the Women's Armed Services Act mandated that there were to be no separate women's branches in the U.S. armed forces. As a result, Willoughby received a regular navy commission.

Source: Kane, Nathan Joseph, *Famous First Facts.* New York: Wilson, 1981, p. 420.

1948 ▪ Geraldine Pratt May (1895-?), an American military officer, was the first director of Women in the Air Force (WAF). The Women's Armed Services Integration Act of 1948

Navel officer Mildred McAfee was the first director of the Women Accepted for Volunteer Emergency Service (WAVES).

declared the WAF a formal part of the U.S. Air Force. May was a graduate of the first Women's Air Corps officer candidate class in 1942.

Source: Read, Phyllis J., and Bernard L. Witlieb, *The Book of Women's Firsts.* New York: Random House, 1992, pp. 272-73.

1950 ▪ **Bernice Rosenthal Walters,** an American physician, became the first female medical doctor assigned to shipboard duty in the U.S. Navy. A lieutenant commander, Walters served with nine other medical officers on board the navy hospital ship, the U.S.S. *Consolation.*

Source: Read, Phyllis J., and Bernard L. Witlieb, *The Book of Women's Firsts.* New York: Random House, 1992, p. 469.

1953 ▪ **Barbara Olive Barnwell,** a staff sergeant in the U.S. Marine Reserve, was the first woman to receive the U.S. Navy-Marine Corps medal for heroism. Barnwell was recognized for her courage in saving private first class Frederick G. Romann from drowning at Camp Lejeune, North Carolina, in 1952.

Source: Kane, Nathan Joseph, *Famous First Facts.* New York: Wilson, 1981, p. 373.

1966 ▪ **Gale Ann Gordon** (1943-), an American naval officer, was the first woman to fly solo as a U.S. Navy pilot. Commissioned as an ensign in the Medical Service Corps at Pensacola Naval Air Station in Florida, Gordon flew a propeller-driven T-34 training aircraft. The only woman in a squadron of 999 men, she began flight training in February 1966. Gordon made her solo flight on March 29, 1966.

Source: Kane, Nathan Joseph, *Famous First Facts.* New York: Wilson, 1981, p. 86.

1969 ▪ **Lieutenant Colonel Frances V. Chaffin** and **Lieutenant Colonel Shirley Rowell Heinze,** both of the Women's Army Corps (WAC), became the first two women to graduate from the U.S. Army War College at Carlisle, Pennsylvania. The Army War College was created in 1901 to provide army officers with instruction in advanced military tactics and strategies.

Source: Kane, Nathan Joseph, *Famous First Facts.* New York: Wilson, 1981, p. 38.

1970 ▪ **Anna Mae Hays** (1920-) and **Elizabeth P. Hoisington** (1918-) shared the honor of being the first women to become U.S. Army generals. Hays was promoted to the rank of brigadier general in the Army Nurse Corps; on the same date, Hoisington was promoted to the same rank in the Women's Army Corps.

Source: Sanders, Dennis, *The First of Everything*. New York: Delacorte Press, 1981, p. 158.

1971 ▪ **Jeanne Marjorie Holm** (1921-), an American military officer, became the first female U.S. Air Force general in Washington, D.C. Holm served at the Pentagon in Washington as director of Women in the Air Force from 1965 until 1972. In 1973 she became the first major general, the highest rank achieved by any woman in the U.S. armed forces. After retiring in 1974, Holm founded "Women in Government" and served as the first chairperson of the organization.

Source: Read, Phyllis J., and Bernard L. Witlieb, *The Book of Women's Firsts*. New York: Random House, 1992, p. 213.

1972 ▪ **Karen Riale** (1949-), an airman in the U.S. Air Force, became the first female member of the U.S. Air Force Band. She joined as a clarinetist. Riale refused to play at the inauguration of President Richard M. Nixon in 1973 because a proper uniform for female band members had not been provided.

Source: Read, Phyllis J., and Bernard L. Witlieb, *The Book of Women's Firsts*. New York: Random House, 1992, p. 366.

1972 ▪ **Alene B. Duerk** (1920-), an American naval officer, was the first woman appointed a rear admiral in the U.S. Navy. Duerk became head of the Navy Nurse Corps in 1970 and in 1972 was promoted from captain to rear admiral. She was the first woman to achieve the rank of admiral in any of the world's navies.

Women Joined Guard

In 1978 five women were appointed to the White House Honor Guard, a group previously consisting of only male military personnel. Representing each of the five branches the U.S. armed services, the women took their posts on May 17, 1978, at the White House in Washington, D.C. The female guards' assignment came about through the efforts of First Lady Rosalynn Carter, wife of President Jimmy Carter, who responded to a letter she had received protesting the exclusion of women.

From 1972-1977 Margaret Brewer served as the last director of the Women Marines.

Source: Read, Phyllis J., and Bernard L. Witlieb, *The Book of Women's Firsts.* New York: Random House, 1992, pp. 126-27.

1973 ▪ **Reba C. Tyler,** a U.S. Army captain, was the first woman to command a North Atlantic Treaty Organization (NATO) military unit. Tyler was appointed to this position in Mannheim, Germany, where she was in charge of the Forty-eighth Adjutant General Postal Detachment.

Source: Read, Phyllis J.,, and Bernard L. Witlieb, *The Book of Women's Firsts.* New York: Random House, 1992, p. 455.

1973 ▪ **Sister Elizabeth M. Edmonds** (1941-), an American Catholic nun, was the first nun to serve as a U.S. Navy officer. Edmonds was commissioned a first lieutenant on her graduation from the University of Pennsylvania Medical School in Philadelphia in 1973.

Source: Read, Phyllis J., and Bernard L. Witlieb, *The Book of Women's Firsts.* New York: Random House, 1992, p. 139.

1974 ▪ **Barbara Rainey** (1948-1982), an American pilot, became the first woman to serve as a pilot in the U.S. Navy. Rainey had a promising career as a naval pilot until her sudden death from unspecified causes while on active duty.

Source: Read, Phyllis J., and Bernard L. Witlieb, *The Book of Women's Firsts,* New York: Random House, 1992, pp. 356-57.

1976 ▪ **Joice Nhongo** (1955-), a Zimbabwe guerilla fighter, was the first woman appointed Camp Commander of Chimoio, the largest guerrilla and refugee camp in Mozambique. Nhongo soon became the most famous fighter in Robert Mugabe's forces. After the creation of Zimbabwe, she served in the new government as Minister of Community Development and Women's Affairs.

Source: Uglow, Jennifer S., ed., *The Continuum Dictionary of Women's Biography,* New York: Continuum, 1989, pp. 400-401.

1978 ▪ Margaret A. Brewer (1930-), an American marine officer, became the first female brigadier general in the U.S. Marine Corps. Brewer served as director of information at marine headquarters in Washington, D.C. The Marine Corps was the last of the armed services in the United States to promote a woman to the rank of general. From 1972-1977 Brewer served as the last director of the Women Marines.

Source: Read, Phyllis J., and Bernard L. Witlieb, *The Book of Women's Firsts*. New York: Random House, 1992, p. 67.

1978 ▪ Mary Clarke (1924-), an American military officer, was the first woman to be promoted to the rank of major general in the U.S. Army. She was also the commander of the Women's Army Corps (WAC) when it was dissolved in 1978. Clarke was the top-ranking female soldier when she retired after 36 years of service.

Source: Read, Phyllis J., and Bernard L. Witlieb, *The Book of Women's Firsts*. New York: Random House, 1992, pp. 92-93.

In 1980 Beverly Kelley and her crew received a Coast Guard citation for rescuing 12 people from sinking boats during a four-day storm.

1979 ▪ Beverly Gwinn Kelley (1952-), a coast guard officer, became the first woman to command a U.S. Coast Guard vessel at sea. From April 1979 through July 1981, Kelley commanded a Coast Guard patrol boat off the coast of Hawaii. In 1980 Kelley and her crew received a Coast Guard citation for rescuing 12 people from sinking or endangered boats during a four-day storm.

Source: Read, Phyllis J., and Bernard L. Witlieb, *The Book of Women's Firsts*. New York: Random House, 1992, p. 238.

c. 1980 ▪ Valérie André (1922-), a French physician, was the first woman to become a general in the French army. André began her military career in 1948 as the chief of medicine of a women's infirmary (medical center) in Vietnam. She went on

Gallina Became Commander

In 1991 Juliane Gallina (1970-), an American naval officer, was the first woman named brigade commander at the U.S. Naval Academy in Annapolis, Maryland. In this capacity, Gallina led the 4,300 members of the brigade, presided at ceremonies, and acted as a liaison between students and academy officers.

to an illustrious career that included service in Algeria. André received numerous honors, including the Légion d'Honneur (Legion of Honor), Croix de Guerre (War Cross), and the U.S. Legion of Merit.

Source: Uglow, Jennifer S., ed., *The Continuum Dictionary of Women's Biography.* New York: Continuum, 1989, p. 17.

1985 ▪ Gail M. Reals (1937-), an American marine officer, was the first woman promoted to the rank of brigadier general in direct competition with men. Reals's distinguished career in the U.S. Marine Corps began in 1956 and ended with her retirement in 1990.

Source: Read, Phyllis J., and Bernard L. Witlieb, *The Book of Women's Firsts.* New York: Random House, 1992, p. 361.

1994 ▪ Kara S. Hultgreen (1965-1994), an American pilot, was the first woman assigned to fly an F-14 fighter jet in combat for the U.S. Navy. Lieutenant Hultgreen ranked third in a class of seven pilots. She was killed on October 25, 1994, during a failed landing on an aircraft carrier.

Source: "Navy Pilot's Body Found," *The New York Times.* November 17, 1994, p. B13.

1994 ▪ Shannon Workman, a naval officer, became the first woman to qualify as a combat-ready naval pilot. As a lieutenant in the U.S. Navy, Workman completed her final requirements by landing on the ship U.S.S. *Eisenhower* off the Virginia coast.

Source: "Navy Women Bringing New Era on Carriers," *The New York Times.* February 21, 1994, p. A1.

Religion

Founders and Leaders
Ordinations and Canonizations

Founders and Leaders

9th century B.C. ▪ Sammuramat (or Semiramis) (c. 800 B.C.-?), an Assyrian queen, developed the cult of the god Nabu. After ruling for 42 years, Sammuramat became the focus of more stories than any other figure in Assyrian history. According to one legend, she was the powerful Semiramis, daughter of a goddess, who irrigated Babylon and conducted numerous military campaigns to expand her territory.

Source: Uglow, Jennifer S., ed., *The Continuum Dictionary of Women's Biography.* New York: Continuum, 1989, p. 476.

C. A.D. 100 ▪ Thecla (1st century), a Christian living in Turkey, was considered the first woman to preach and to baptize converts to Christianity. A follower of Paul, one of the apostles (preachers), Thecla was responsible for converting many women to Christianity during the first century.

Source: Chicago, Judy, *The Dinner Party.* New York: Anchor, 1979, p. 132.

Evangeline Booth was the first commander of the Salvation Army. (See "Founders and Leaders" entry dated 1840s.)

The Mother Goddess

Nearly all early cultures regarded a woman as the source of life. In Babylonia, Tiamat was "She Who Gave Birth To All." The Inuits (native peoples in present-day Alaska) worshiped Sedna, the Creator and Protector. For the Greeks, Gaea (or Gaia) was Mother Earth, and in India the primary deity was Kāl_, who gave birth to all beings. Egyptians paid tribute to Nut and her daughter Isis as the source of life. Inanna was the great goddess of the Syrians. In Germany, Nerthus was Mother Earth.

C. A.D. 355 ▪ Macrina (327-379), a Turkish physician and Christian leader, founded a women's community in Asia Minor (now an area principally in Turkey). According to an early text, life in her monastery was based on "no hatred, pride, luxuries, or honor." Macrina also founded a pioneering hospital at Cappadoc in Turkey. An active member of the early Christian Church, she was later declared a saint with her brothers, the bishops Gregory and Basil.

Source: Chicago, Judy, *The Dinner Party*. New York: Anchor, 1979, p. 134.

6th century ▪ Bertha of England (?-612), an English queen, founded the first Christian church in England. When Bertha, a French princess, married the king of Kent, she insisted that her marriage contract give her the right to practice Christianity. She established a church at Canterbury, which then began its long history as the spiritual center of England. According to some historians, Bertha was also instrumental in producing the first written English laws.

Source: Chicago, Judy, *The Dinner Party*. New York: Anchor, 1979, p. 130.

C. A.D. 500 ▪ St. Brigid (or Bridget) (453-523), a patron saint of Ireland, is believed to have founded the first convent in Ireland at Kildare. Although Brigid is reported to have lived from 453 to 523, her actual existence has been debated. Some scholars believe Brigid was a Christianization of the Celtic moon goddess Bridgit. (The Celts were people who settled the British Isles from 2,000 to 200 B.C.) Kildare was the site of a shrine to the goddess Bridgit, who was celebrated with a feast and fires on February 1. Similarly, St. Brigid's feast day is February 1, and is also celebrated by the lighting of fires. The nuns at the Kildare convent are said to have tended a sacred fire (which no man was allowed to approach) for many generations.

Source: Uglow, Jennifer S., ed., *The Continuum Dictionary of Women's Biography*. New York: Continuum, 1989, p. 87.

A.D. 610 ▪ **Khadijah** (564-619), the Arabian first wife of Muhammad, supported the prophet after his first vision. (Muhammad was the founder of Islam.) A successful business-woman in the Meccan tribe of Quraish, Khadijah married Muhammad in A.D. 604 and encouraged him in his mission to spread his new religion. Although Muhammad went on to have 11 more wives, he remained faithful to Khadijah during her lifetime. According to the Koran (the sacred text of Islam), she is one of the "four perfect women."

Source: Uglow, Jennifer S., ed., *The Continuum Dictionary of Women's Biography.* New York: Continuum, 1989, p. 298.

631 ▪ **A'ishah Bint Abi Bakr** (613-678), an Arabian Muslim leader, is considered the first woman authority on Muslim tradition. She was the favorite wife of Muhammad, the prophet and founder of Islam (the Muslim religion). After his death in 631, A'ishah emerged as a powerful religious leader in the ensuing political turmoil. Her teachings contributed to the emergence of the Sunni Muslims (a branch of Islam that advocates following the original teachings of Muhammad).

Source: Uglow, Jennifer S., ed., *The Continuum Dictionary of Women's Biography.* New York: Continuum, 1989, p. 11.

659 ▪ **Hilda of Whitby** (616-680), an English nun, was the founder of an important monastery at Whitby, England. As abbess (head administrator), she presided over one of the first Christian monasteries to house women and men in adjoining quarters. Among the inhabitants were St. John of Beverley and Caedmon, the first English religious poet. Five of the monks who were at Whitby during Hilda's tenure went on to become bishops. A strong and influential leader, Hilda was later made a saint.

Source: Uglow, Jennifer S., ed., *The Continuum Dictionary of Women's Biography.* New York: Continuum, 1989, p. 259.

Late tenth century ▪ **Adelaide** (931-999), a French noble-woman, was the founder of the Cluniac monastery at Selz in Alsace, France. (The Cluniacs were a Roman Catholic religious order related to the Benedictines, who devoted themselves to worship and work.) An Italian queen and empress, Adelaide influenced the rules of her husbands, Lothair of Italy and Otto I of Germany, as well as her sons, Otto II and Otto III. She is remembered particularly for her contributions to the development of monasteries during the medieval period. Adelaide was made a saint in 1097.

Source: Uglow, Jennifer S., ed., *The Continuum Dictionary of Women's Biography.* New York: Continuum, 1989, p. 6.

Twelfth century ▪ Hildegard of Bingen (1098-1178) was founder and first abbess of the convent at Bingen in Germany. She was also the first woman to compose hymns for the Mass (Roman Catholic church service). A learned woman who was also an accomplished artist and musician, Hildegard wrote books on natural history and medicine. She was a famous visionary (one who sees supernatural beings that reveal truth), whose revelations began in 1130.

Source: Uglow, Jennifer S., ed., *The Continuum Dictionary of Women's Biography.* New York: Continuum, 1989, pp. 259-60.

1147 ▪ Eleanor of Aquitaine (1122-1204), queen of France and England, led a Crusade to the Holy Land. (The Crusades were military expeditions undertaken by the Christian church from the eleventh through the thirteenth centuries to win the Holy Land from the Muslims.) Eleanor organized 300 women, known as the Queen's Amazons, and prepared them to fight and tend wounded soldiers during the ill-fated journey to the East. The failure of this Crusade ultimately led to Eleanor's divorce from Louis VII (1120-1180) of France. She later married Henry II (1133-1189) of England, whom she helped attain the crown.

Source: Chicago, Judy, *The Dinner Party.* New York: Anchor, 1979, pp. 74-75.

Early thirteenth century ▪ Clare of Assisi (1194-1253), an Italian religious leader, founded the "Poor Clares." The female counterpart to the Franciscan Order, the community was established by St. Francis at Assisi. Clare was the first abbess (head of the order), and she and her female followers lived in poverty like the Franciscan monks. The Clares had a significant influence on the church and society during the early thirteenth century.

Source: Uglow, Jennifer S., ed., *The Continuum Dictionary of Women's Biography.* New York: Continuum, 1989, p. 126.

Early fourteenth century ▪ Elizabeth of Portugal (1271-1336), a French-born Portuguese queen, was founder of the Convent of the Poor Clares at Coimbra in Portugal. She retired to the convent after the death of her husband, King Dinis, in 1325. Elizabeth was canonized (declared a saint) in 1625 for her work on behalf of the poor and the sick.

Source: Uglow, Jennifer S., ed., *The Continuum Dictionary of Women's Biography.* New York: Continuum, 1989, p. 189.

1370 ▪ Bridget Godmarsson (1303-1373), a Swedish noble-woman and saint, founded the Order of the Holy Savior or the "Bridgetines." Commanded in a revelation (or vision) to found a new religious order, Bridget was given approval to do so by the pope (the head of the Roman Catholic Church) in 1370. She spent most of her life in Rome, Italy, where she tended the poor and sick. Bridget was canonized (declared a saint) in 1391 and became the patron saint of Sweden.

Source: Uglow, Jennifer S., ed., *The Continuum Dictionary of Women's Biography.* New York: Continuum, 1989, p. 87.

1535 ▪ Angela Merici (Angela of Brescia) (1474-1540), an Italian saint, founded the first women's teaching order in the Catholic Church. She established the Company of St. Ursula to educate girls and to give them individual attention. Although the girls continued to live in their own homes, they took vows of virginity, poverty, and obedience. They also performed good deeds for their families and neighbors. The Church did not officially approve the order until 1565. Angela was canonized (elevated to sainthood) in 1807.

Source: Chicago, Judy, *The Dinner Party.* New York: Anchor, 1979, p. 151.

Teresa of Ávila, a Spanish saint, founded St. Joseph's convent at Ávila.

1562 ▪ Teresa of Ávila (1515-1582), a Spanish saint, founded St. Joseph's convent at Ávila. Part of the Carmelite order (originally a community of mystics who lived as hermits), St. Joseph's was organized according strict self-discipline, poverty, and daily prayer. Teresa went on to found 17 other Carmelite convents in Spain. She combined a life of contemplation with practical activity and became, along with St. Catherine of Siena, one of the first two women to be officially declared a Doctor of the Church, in 1970.

Source: Uglow, Jennifer S., ed., *The Continuum Dictionary of Women's Biography.* New York: Continuum, 1989, p. 535.

c. 1610 ▪ Mary Joan Ward (1585-1645), an English Roman Catholic, was the founder of the "English Ladies." Members of this lay pastoral order (women who did not take religious vows) worked in the community and paid particular attention to women's needs. In 1621 English Catholic leaders appealed to the pope to order the dissolution of the group, arguing that women were unsuited to pastoral work. In 1629 the "English Ladies" was finally suppressed. Ward is also remembered as a founder of schools for girls and for the poor in France, Italy, Germany, Austria, and Hungary.

Source: Uglow, Jennifer S., ed., *The Continuum Dictionary of Women's Biography.* New York: Continuum, 1989, p. 569.

1633 ▪ Louise de Marillac (1591-1660), a French aristocrat, founded the order of the Daughters of Charity. The Daughters cared for orphaned and poor children, galley slaves (people who worked the oars of ships), the elderly, and the insane. Canonized (declared a saint) in 1934, Louise was named the patron saint of social workers by Pope John XXIII.

Source: Uglow, Jennifer S., ed., *The Continuum Dictionary of Women's Biography.* New York: Continuum, 1989, p. 158.

1635 ▪ **Anne Hutchinson** (1591-1643) was the first person to disagree with New England Puritan orthodoxy (the religious laws of a strict Christian denomination). She met with Puritans in her home in Boston, Massachusetts, to discuss both secular and theological issues and questioned what she saw as the Puritan emphasis on salvation (deliverance from sin) through good works. Instead, Hutchinson argued for salvation through grace (forgiveness of sins) and for a direct relation with God. For speaking out, Hutchinson was tried, excommunicated, and banished from the colony in 1638.

Source: Read, Phyllis J., and Bernard L. Witlieb, *The Book of Women's Firsts*. New York: Random House, 1992, pp. 222-23.

1727 ▪ **Marie Tranchepain** (?-1733), a French Roman Catholic nun, established the first permanent convent in what would become the United States. Arriving from France with twelve other Ursuline nuns (members of the Company of St. Ursula), Tranchepain—as the mother superior (head of the order)—built a convent in New Orleans, Louisiana. Originally the convent consisted of a small, two-story wooden building in the French Quarter of New Orleans, from which the sisters also ran their school for girls. The convent and gardens, rebuilt in 1750, still stand. The sisters and their school, called the Ursuline Academy, eventually moved to larger quarters a few blocks north of the original site.

Source: McCullough, Joan, *First of All: Significant "Firsts" by American Women.* New York: Holt, 1980, pp. 106-07.

1766 ▪ **Barbara Ruckie Heck** (1734-1804), an Irish-born religious leader, cofounded, with her cousin, Phillip Embury, the Methodist Church in the United States. (The Methodist Church is a Protestant Christian denomination, founded by British theologian John Wesley [1703-1791], that stresses per-

Anne Hutchinson was the first person to disagree with Puritan laws.

sonal and social morality.) Settling in New York City, Heck organized services for the first Methodist Society. She also supervised construction of a building, the John Street Methodist Church, which still stands in New York. Heck later moved with her husband to Sorel, Canada, where she established another Methodist Society.

Source: Read, Phyllis J., and Bernard L. Witlieb, *The Book of Women's Firsts.* New York: Random House, 1992, p. 199.

1774 ▪ **Ann Lee** (1736-1784), an English religious leader, established the first Shaker group in the United States. (The Shakers are a Christian religious group that advocates leading a simple life in a close-knit community and refraining from sexual relations. The name "Shakers" derived from the group members' behavior during worship service, when they shake and tremble.) After experiencing a vision that directed her to start a community of Shakers (officially called the "United Society of Believers in Christ's Second Appearing") in New England, Lee and a group of followers settled in New York state. Believing that Jesus (the founder of Christianity) would return as a woman, the Shakers advocated equal rights for women.

Lee was also remembered for becoming the first leader of conscientious objectors (people who oppose war on religious or moral grounds) when she spoke out against the Revolutionary War in 1780. (The Revolutionary War was a movement by American colonists to gain independence from British rule.) Lee was eventually jailed as a traitor and then released.

Source: James, Edward T., and others, *Notable American Women, 1607-1950: A Biographical Dictionary.* Cambridge, Massachusetts: Harvard University Press, 1971, pp. 385-87.

1794 ▪ **Jemima Wilkinson** (1752-1819), an American religious leader, founded Jerusalem Township, a community near Keuka Lake, New York. After having visions in her youth, Wilkinson named herself "The Public Universal Friend." With a number of followers who were eager to establish a utopian community (or perfect society), she funded exploration of Genesee County, New York, in the 1780s and continued to encourage western settlement throughout her life.

Source: James, Edward T., and others, *Notable American Women, 1607-1950: A Biographical Dictionary.* Cambridge, Massachusetts: Harvard University Press, 1971, pp. 609-10.

1809 ▪ Elizabeth Ann Bayley Seton

(1774-1821), an American nun, was the founder of the first Catholic order in the United States. Known as Mother Seton, she established the Sisters of Charity of St. Joseph, which was devoted to poor relief and education. Seton is credited with starting parochial (religious) schools in the United States. She became the first American-born saint in 1975.

Source: James, Edward T., and others, *Notable American Women, 1607-1950: A Biographical Dictionary.* Cambridge, Massachusetts: Harvard University Press, 1971, pp. 263-65.

1812 ▪ Ann Hasseltine Judson (1789-

1826) was the first U.S. woman to become a foreign missionary. Judson set out with her husband from Salem, Massachusetts, in 1812 and arrived in Rangoon, Burma, the following year. Except for a few trips west for her health, she remained in Burma until her death. Working to convert the local people to Christianity, Judson lived through tumultuous circumstances brought on by British colonialism in the area.

In 1975 Elizabeth Seton became the first American-born saint.

Source: James, Edward T., and others, *Notable American Women, 1607-1950: A Biographical Dictionary.* Cambridge, Massachusetts: Harvard University Press, 1971, pp. 295-97.

1818 ▪ Rose Philippine Duchesne (1769-1862), a French-

born American nun, was the founder of the American convents of the Sacred Heart. She opened the first convent in St. Charles, Missouri, in 1818. Neither this convent nor the one opened the following year in Florissant prospered, however. The first successful Sacred Heart convent was at Grand Coteau, Louisiana, in 1821. Duchesne was canonized a saint in 1988.

Source: James, Edward T., and others, *Notable American Women, 1607-1950: A Biographical Dictionary.* Cambridge, Massachusetts: Harvard University Press, 1971, pp. 524-26.

1838 ▪ Rebecca Gratz (1781-1869), an American community activist, founded the first Hebrew Sunday School. She established the Hebrew Sunday School Society in 1838 in Philadelphia, Pennsylvania. Gratz devoted her life to charity work and religion, emphasizing the needs of women and children.

Source: Read, Phyllis J., and Bernard L. Witlieb, *The Book of Women's Firsts.* New York: Random House, 1992, p. 184.

1840s ▪ Catherine Mumford Booth (1829-1890), an English religious leader, was the cofounder—with her husband, William Booth—of the Salvation Army. The couple's work preaching on London street corners in the 1840s led to their rejection of conventional Wesleyan Methodism (a Protestant Christian denomination founded by English theologian John Wesley [1703- 1791], which stressed personal and social morality). In 1865 the Booths' new, militant Christian organization became known as the Salvation Army.

The Booths' daughter, **Evangeline Booth,** the first female commander of the organization, carried on her parents' work in the United States in the early 1900s. The Salvation Army always treated women equitably (fairly) within its organization; if a marriage occurs between two Salvation Army officers, the one with the lower rank is always promoted to the higher rank, so that the partners work together at the same level.

Source: James, Edward T., and others, *Notable American Women, 1607-1950: A Biographical Dictionary.* Cambridge, Massachusetts: Harvard University Press, 1971, pp. 204-06.

1847 ▪ Cornelia Augusta Connelly (1809-1879), an American Roman Catholic nun, was the founder and first head of the Society of the Holy Child Jesus, in Derby, England. Connelly led a dramatic life. Persuaded by her husband to convert to Catholicism and take religious vows, she founded the Society of the Holy Child Jesus. In the meantime her husband, who became a Catholic priest, removed their children from her care and tried to take control of her new society. Then he renounced his vows and sought to restore his conjugal rights by court action (conjugal rights refer to those implied by the status of marriage, including those pertaining to sexuality). The court ruled in his favor in 1849, but was overturned on appeal in 1851 in a much publicized case.

Source: James, Edward T., and others, *Notable American Women, 1607-1950: A Biographical Dictionary.* Cambridge, Massachusetts: Harvard University Press, 1971, pp. 373-75.

1852 ▪ Benedicta Riepp (1825-1862), an American-born Roman Catholic nun, founded the Sisters of Saint Benedict in the United States. Riepp left Europe in 1852 and began the order with three sisters at the German colony of St. Mary's in Elk County, Pennsylvania. The Sisters of Saint Benedict has prospered in America and is dedicated to teaching and to maintaining orphanages, hospitals, and nursing homes for the ill and aged.

Source: James, Edward T., and others, *Notable American Women, 1607-1950: A Biographical Dictionary.* Cambridge, Massachusetts: Harvard University Press, 1971, pp. 160-61.

Miki Founded Tenrikyo

In 1858 Nakayama Miki (1798-1887), a Japanese religious leader, founded the "Tenrikyo" religion. From childhood Miki worshiped Shinto deities. (The national religion of Japan, Shinto is devoted to the worship of gods of nature.) At the age of 40, however, Miki had a vision that told her to give away all of her family's possessions to needy people. Twenty years later, Miki began faith healing (the practice of curing diseases and disabilities through religious faith). At that time she also founded the religion Tenrikyo, and taught her disciples dances to perform before God. Tenrikyo is still practiced today.

1855 ▪ Angela Gillespie (1824-1887), an American Roman Catholic nun, founded the Sisters of the Holy Cross. At the time a small community of French sisters existed at Notre Dame University and at St. Mary's Academy in Bertrand, Michigan. Gillespie moved St. Mary's to South Bend, Indiana, in 1855 and developed the order. The school soon became St. Mary's College under her leadership. Nearly forty other schools had been established under Gillespie's auspices by the time of her death.

Source: James, Edward T., and others, *Notable American Women, 1607-1950: A Biographical Dictionary.* Cambridge, Massachusetts: Harvard University Press, 1971, pp. 34-35.

1863 ▪ Ellen Gould Harmon White (1827-1915), an American religious leader, was the cofounder of the Seventh-Day

Adventist Church. (Seventh-Day Adventists believe in the second coming of Christ, and they observe the Sabbath on Saturday.) An itinerant (traveling) preacher and mystic visionary from her youth, she established the church with her husband, James Springer White, in Battle Creek, Michigan. Although the Whites gained followers in the 1840s and 1850s, they did not formalize their religion until 1863. Ellen White also worked for such causes as the abolition (elimination) of slavery and biblical study in higher education.

Source: James, Edward T., and others, *Notable American Women, 1607-1950: A Biographical Dictionary.* Cambridge, Massachusetts: Harvard University Press, 1971, pp. 585-88.

1865 ▪ Harriet Starr Cannon (1823-1896), an American religious leader, was the first mother superior (administrative head) of the Episcopal Community of St. Mary. She and four other women, who elected Cannon as their leader, became the initial members in a service at St. Michael's Church in New York City in 1865. The community worked to feed and shelter the poor and in 1870 established St. Mary's Free Hospital for Poor Children. The group opened St. Mary's School in New York City in 1868 and several others were thereafter established in New York, Tennessee, and Wisconsin. At the time of Cannon's death, the community included 104 sisters.

Source: James, Edward T., and others, *Notable American Women, 1607-1950: A Biographical Dictionary.* Cambridge, Massachusetts: Harvard University Press, 1971, pp. 283-84.

1875 ▪ Helena Petrovna Blavatsky (1831-1891), a Russian-born American spiritualist, was the cofounder of modern theosophy, a system of belief founded on a tradition of spiritualism (a belief that the spirits of the dead communicate with the living) and the occult (the belief in and communication with supernatural powers). Born in Russia, Blavatsky arrived at her beliefs through travels in Turkey, Greece, India, and Tibet. In 1875 she and Henry Steel Olcott founded the Theosophical Society in the United States. Rejecting traditional religion and science, Blavatsky claimed to have psychic powers (the ability to understand and communicate with supernatural forces) and advocated mystical experience as the only way to arrive at truth.

Source: James, Edward T., and others, *Notable American Women, 1607-1950: A Biographical Dictionary.* Cambridge, Massachusetts: Harvard University Press, 1971, pp. 174-77.

1879 ▪ Mary Baker Eddy (1821-1910), an American religious leader, founded the Church of Christ (Scientist), commonly known as Christian Science. (Christian Scientists believe that sin, sickness, and death are only mental states and can be destroyed through study of the Scriptures to understand Jesus's healing powers.) Baker established the Christian Science Association in 1876, and three years later she started the church, both in Boston, Massachusetts. Eddy was inspired to develop Christian Science after she suffered a serious fall and recovered while reading the New Testament of the Christian Bible. In 1883 she founded the *Christian Science Journal* and in 1908 she began publishing *The Christian Science Monitor,* a daily newspaper that still has a wide circulation today.

Source: James, Edward T., and others, *Notable American Women, 1607-1950: A Biographical Dictionary.* Cambridge, Massachusetts: Harvard University Press, 1971, pp. 551-61.

1887 ▪ Lucy Jane Rider Meyer (1849-1922), an American leader of the Methodist Church, was the first successful advocate of the deaconess movement in the United States. The organization encouraged the use of groups of lay women (those who do not take religious vows) for social service work as "deaconesses" (the female counterparts of deacons, who are male church leaders). An 1872 graduate of Oberlin College, Meyer organized the first American deaconess home in Chicago, Illinois, in 1887. Members of deaconess groups adopted a distinctive costume, a black dress with white collar and cuffs. The following year the organization was recognized by the Methodist Episcopal Church.

Source: James, Edward T., and others, *Notable American Women, 1607-1950: A Biographical Dictionary.* Cambridge, Massachusetts: Harvard University Press, 1971, pp. 534-36.

1897 ▪ **Ursula Newell Gestefeld** (1845-1921), founded and was first president of the Exodus Club, in Chicago, Illinois. Gestefeld developed her own religious system after splitting with Mary Baker Eddy's Church of Christ (Scientist). (Christian Scientists believe that sin, sickness, and death are only mental states and can be overcome through study of the Scriptures to understand Christ's healing powers.) In 1904 Gestefeld developed the Church of the New Thought and the College of the Science of Being. Emphasizing logic and reasoning rather than an individual figure or church authority, Gestefeld wrote about her ideas in a monthly magazine called *Exodus.* She was the first and only editor of the magazine, which was published between 1896 and 1904.

Source: James, Edward T., and others, *Notable American Women, 1607-1950: A Biographical Dictionary.* Cambridge, Massachusetts: Harvard University Press, 1971, pp. 27-28.

1901 ▪ **Alma Bridwell White** (1862-1946), an American religious leader, was the first female bishop of any Christian church. In 1901 she founded the fundamentalist Methodist sect that became known after 1917 as the "Pillar of Fire Church." (The Methodist church is a Protestant Christian denomination founded by the English theologian John Wesley [1703-1791], which stressed individual and social morality. A fundamentalist sect is a small religious group that believes in the literal interpretation of religious texts, in this case the Bible.) As head of this religion, White held the title of bishop (one who supervises ministers and other clergy). A tireless traveler and preacher both in America and Europe, White founded seven schools, among them the Alma White College in New Jersey in 1921. In 1932 she took up painting, producing over three hundred mountain landscapes in a primitive folk style (a painting technique that uses simple shapes and primary colors). White was also a prolific author, writing a five-volume autobiography, two radio dramas, several volumes of poetry, and over two hundred hymns.

Source: James, Edward T., and others, *Notable American Women, 1607-1950: A Biographical Dictionary.* Cambridge, Massachusetts: Harvard University Press, 1971, pp. 581-83.

1920 ▪ **Mary Joseph Rogers** (1882-1955), an American Roman Catholic leader, founded the Maryknoll Sisters of St. Dominic in Ossining, New York. Devoted to foreign missions, the group was originally called the "Foreign Mission Sisters of St. Dominic." Known as Mother Mary Joseph, Rogers served as the organization's president from 1925 until her retirement in 1947.

Source: Read, Phyllis J., and Bernard L. Witlieb, *The Book of Women's Firsts.* New York: Random House, 1992, pp. 376-77.

1923 ▪ **Alice Mildred Cable** (1878-1952) and her friends Evangeline French (1869-1960) and Francesca French (1871-1960), who were American missionaries, became the first women to be granted permission from the Chinese government to preach to the nomadic tribes in the Gobi Desert. The women devoted their lives to missionary work in the Far East and to careful observations of geography during their travels.

Source: Uglow, Jennifer S., ed., *The Continuum Dictionary of Women's Biography.* New York: Continuum, 1989, p. 101.

1923 ▪ **Aimée Semple McPherson** (1890-1944), a Canadian evangelist, founded the International Church of the Foursquare Gospel, in Los Angeles, California. McPherson was initially active in the Salvation Army (a religious social service organization based on a military structure). She then served as a missionary in Asia after her marriage to Robert Semple, a Pentecostal evangelist. (Pentecostalism is a form of Christianity that emphasizes one's individual spiritual gifts, expressive worship, and the literal interpretation of the four Gospels of the Bible.) After her husband's death in 1910, McPherson began an evangelical (missionary) crusade across the United States, preaching the Foursquare Gospel. McPherson taught that Jesus (the founder of Christianity) had four roles: savior, baptizer, healer, and future king. Faith healing also played a major role in the church. McPherson had a large following during the 1920s and 1930s and led a dramatic life; she died of an overdose of sleeping pills.

Source: Uglow, Jennifer S., ed., *The Continuum Dictionary of Women's Biography.* New York: Continuum, 1989, p. 348.

Mother Teresa of Calcutta founded the Order of the Missionaries of Charity.

1930 ▪ **Gladys Aylward** (1903-1970), an English missionary, and a Scotswoman named Miss Dawson, founded "The Inn of the Sixth Happiness." It was a hotel in China at which local travelers were taught the gospel (the message of Jesus Christ, the founder of Christianity). After becoming a Chinese citizen in 1931, Aylward did not return to England until 1948. She then went back to Taiwan in 1953 to work with refugees and orphans. A film based on her experiences, called *The Inn of the Sixth Happiness,* starring Ingrid Bergman, was made in 1958.

Source: Uglow, Jennifer S., ed., *The Continuum Dictionary of Women's Biography.* New York: Continuum, 1989, p. 38.

1950 ▪ **Mother Teresa of Calcutta (given name, Agnes Bojaxhiu;** 1910-1997), a Yugoslavian Roman Catholic nun, founded the Order of the Missionaries of Charity. In 1928 she joined the Sisters of Loretto, a Roman Catholic religious order, as a teacher in Calcutta, India. Three years later Agnes took the name Teresa in honor of Saint Teresa of Ávila; she became a nun in 1937. Mother Teresa left the convent in 1947 to open a school for destitute (extremely poor) children in the slums of Calcutta. In 1979 she was awarded the Nobel Peace Prize for her work. In recent years the Missionaries of Charity has expanded to over two hundred centers in several countries for the treatment of lepers, the blind, the disabled, the aged, and the dying.

Source: Parry, Melanie, ed., *Larousse Dictionary of Women.* New York: Larousse Kingfisher Chambers, Inc., 1995, p. 641.

1960 ▪ **Fayvelle Mermey** (1916-1977), an American religious activist, was the first woman to serve as president of a synagogue (a Jewish house of worship). She headed the Larchmont Temple in suburban New York City for two terms, 1960-1962 and 1972-1974. Her election in 1960 was widely noted as evidence of the equality of women with men in temple administration in Reform Judaism (a liberal approach to the observance of traditional laws of the Jewish religion).

Source: O'Neill, Lois Decker, ed., *The Women's Book of World Records and Achievements.* New York: Doubleday, 1979, p. 395.

1974 ▪ Claire Randall (1919-), an American religious leader, became the first woman to serve as secretary (director) of the National Council of Churches of Christ. (The Churches of Christ is a conservative body of Protestant Christians who believe in the literal interpretation of the Bible, especially the four Gospels.) Randall worked towards ecumenism (cooperation among religions), especially between Protestants and Roman Catholics.

Source: Read, Phyllis J., and Bernard L. Witlieb, *The Book of Women's Firsts.* New York: Random House, 1992, p. 359.

1982 ▪ Cynthia L. Hale (1952-), an American religious leader, was the first woman to be elected head of the Disciples of Christ. (The Disciples of Christ is a Protestant Christian body that believes the Bible alone is the basis of faith and individual conduct, and that each person is free to interpret the Scriptures.) Hale achieved this distinction at the National Convocation of the Christian Church in 1982.

Source: *Jet.* August 30, 1982, p. 24.

1995 ▪ Sister Maatje, a Swiss nun, was the first woman to carry the symbolic cross during the pope's Good Friday procession, in Rome, Italy. (Good Friday is the annual anniversary of Jesus's death on the cross.) Sister Maatje was accompanied by Pope John Paul II, who had decided to make this gesture toward including women in Roman Catholic church services.

Source: *The Willoughby (Ohio) News Herald.* April 14, 1995.

Ordinations and Canonizations

A.D. 353 ▪ Marcellina, an Italian Roman Catholic, was the first nun to be recognized by the Christian Church in a religious ceremony held in Rome, Italy. St. Ambrose (A.D. 339-397), Marcellina's brother, wrote *De Virginibus* for her. In this work, Ambrose listed the rules by which nuns were to live.

Source: Chicago, Judy, *The Dinner Party*. New York: Anchor, 1979, p. 130.

1235 ▪ **Olga** (892-971), a Russian princess, was the first Russian to be named a saint in the Eastern Orthodox Church. (The Eastern Orthodox Church observes the doctrines of Roman Catholicism but does not recognize the supreme authority of the pope, who is known as the bishop of Rome.) Olga was the wife of prince Igor of Kiev, and served as co-regent (co-ruler) from 945 to 964 while their son was a minor. She became a Christian in 957 and was baptized at Constantinople (now Istanbul, Turkey). When she returned to Russia, Olga encouraged the spread of Christianity throughout Russia.

Source: Magnusson, Magnus, ed., *Larousse Biographical Dictionary*. Edinburgh: Larousse Kingfisher Chambers, Inc., 1994, p. 1102.

1752 ▪ **Mary Terpin** (1731-1761), an American nun, was the first woman born in the United States to become a nun. Born in Illinois to Canadian and Native-American parents, Terpin went to live and study with the Ursuline sisters (a Roman Catholic religious order) in New Orleans, Louisiana, when she was 17. A year later she became a postulant (a probationary candidate for consecration as a nun). Upon taking her final vows in 1752, Terpin became Sister St. Martha and spent the rest of her brief life at the convent.

Source: McCullough, Joan, *First of All: Significant "Firsts" by American Women*. New York: Holt, 1980, p. 106.

1853 ▪ **Antoinette Brown** (1825-1921), an American religious leader and feminist, was the first woman in the United States to become an ordained minister. The ordination (official ceremony) took place at the First Congregational Church in Butler, New York. (In the Congregational Church, a Protestant Christian denomination, the local congregation is independent from a central church government.) As a result of theological differences, however, Brown withdrew as a minister of the church the following year and became a Unitarian. (The Unitarian Church is a Protestant Christian denomination that believes the deity exists only in one person, as opposed to the traditional Christian belief in the trinity: the father [God], son [Jesus of Nazareth], and the holy spirit.)

Source: Read, Phyllis J., and Bernard L. Witlieb, *The Book of Women's Firsts*. New York: Random House, 1992, p. 70.

1863 ▪ Olympia Brown (1835-1926), an American religious leader and feminist, was the first woman ordained a Universalist minister. (The Universalist church is a Protestant Christian denomination that believes all human beings will eventually be saved from sin.) Brown was ordained in Malone, New York. A graduate of Antioch College and the theological school of St. Lawrence University, Brown became a charter member of the American Equal Rights Association in 1866. She resigned her pastorate in Racine, Wisconsin, to devote herself to the cause of women's suffrage (a campaign for the right to vote) in 1887.

Olympia Brown was the first woman ordained as a Universalist minister.

Source: James, Edward T., and others, eds., *Notable American Women, 1607-1950: A Biographical Dictionary*. Cambridge, Massachusetts: Harvard University Press, 1971, pp. 256-58.

1871 ▪ Celia C. Burleigh (1827-1875), an American religious leader and feminist, was the first woman ordained as a minister in the Unitarian Church. (The Unitarian church is a Protestant Christian denomination that believes the deity exists only in one person, as opposed to the traditional Christian belief in the trinity: the father [God], son [Jesus of Nazareth], and the holy spirit.) She served at a parish in Brooklyn, Connecticut. Burleigh was a woman's suffrage advocate (one who supports women's right to vote) throughout her life.

Source: Read, Phyllis J., and Bernard L. Witlieb, *The Book of Women's Firsts*. New York: Random House, 1992, p. 76.

1946 ▪ **Frances Xavier Cabrini** (1850-1917), an Italian-born American Roman Catholic nun, was the first United States citizen to be named a saint in the Roman Catholic Church. Cabrini founded a new religious order, the Missionary Sisters of the Sacred Heart, in Italy in 1880. Pope Leo XIII sent Cabrini to the United States in 1889 to work with Italian immigrants. She eventually became known as "Mother Cabrini" for her charitable work, which included founding more than 67 shelters in the United States; she also set up shelters in Buenos Aires, Argentina; Paris, France; and Madrid, Spain. Cabrini was canonized (declared a saint) in 1946. Her feast (commemoration) day is November 13.

Source: James, Edward T., and others, eds., *Notable American Women, 1607-1950: A Biographical Dictionary.* Cambridge, Massachusetts: Harvard University Press, 1971, pp. 274-76.

1965 ▪ **Rachel Henderlite** (1905-), an American church leader, was the first woman ordained as an American Presbyterian minister. (The Presbyterian Church, which was founded by French religious reformer John Calvin [1509-1564], is a Protestant Christian denomination that is governed by representative bodies that have legislative and judicial powers. Presbyterians believe that people are born as sinful beings and that human fate is predetermined by God.) Henderlite continued to be active in church service and administration throughout her life.

Source: James, Edward T., and others, eds., *Notable American Women, 1607-1950: A Biographical Dictionary.* Cambridge, Massachusetts: Harvard University Press, 1971, p. 200.

1970 ▪ **Barbara Andrews** (1934-1978), an American Protestant minister, was the first woman to be ordained as a minister in the American Lutheran Church.(The first Protestant Christian denomination, the Lutheran Church was founded by German theologian Martin Luther [1483-1546]. It is based on the belief that a person's religious commitment is determined by faith in God alone and not by obedience to church authorities.) Andrews began her ministry in 1970 in Minneapolis, Minnesota, and at the time of her death was acting pastor of Resurrection Lutheran Church in Detroit, Michigan.

Source: Read, Phyllis J., and Bernard L. Witlieb, *The Book of Women's Firsts.* New York: Random House, 1992, p. 20.

1972 ▪ Sally Priesand (1946-), an American rabbi, was the first American woman ordained in Reform Judaism. (Reform Judaism is the liberal approach to the observance of traditional laws of the Jewish religion.) Ordained in Cincinnati, Ohio, Priesand went on to serve as rabbi (the official leader of a Jewish religious congregation) in various other congregations in New York and New Jersey.

Source: Read, Phyllis J., and Bernard L. Witlieb, *The Book of Women's Firsts.* New York: Random House, 1992, p. 350.

1975 ▪ Barbara Herman (1952-), an American Jewish religious leader, became the first female cantor in American Reform Judaism when she was chosen to serve in this capacity at Shalom Temple of Clifton-Passaic, New Jersey. (A cantor is a synagogue official who sings or chants music and leads the congregation in prayer during a Jewish religious service. Reform Judaism is the liberal approach to the observance of traditional laws of the Jewish religion.) Herman graduated from a five-year program for cantors at the School of Sacred Music, Hebrew Union College-Jewish Institute of Religion in New York City.

Source: Read, Phyllis J., and Bernard L. Witlieb, *The Book of Women's Firsts.* New York: Random House, 1992, p. 202.

1977 ▪ Mary Michael Simpson (1926-), an American Protestant Christian leader, was the first woman to become a canon (a priest who assists the dean, or head of a cathedral) in the Episcopal Church. (The Episcopal Church is the American form of the Anglican Church, which is the official religion of Great Britain. The Anglican Church is similar to the Roman Catholic Church, except that the pope is not recognized as the

Catherine Declared Doctor

In 1970 Catherine of Siena (1347-1380; patron saint of Italy), was one of the first two women to be declared a "Doctor of the Roman Catholic Church." (The other woman was Teresa of Ávila, 1515-1582.) Catherine was a mystical visionary who worked as a reformer of the Roman Catholic Church during a turbulent time in its history. Catherine traveled widely with a group of followers, ministering to the poor and winning converts. Despite her vigorous and successful political efforts, however, she was made a saint in 1461 because of her personal faith, charity, and holiness.

ultimate religious authority.) Simpson served in this capacity at the Cathedral of St. John the Divine in New York City from 1977 through 1987.

Source: Read, Phyllis J., and Bernard L. Witlieb, *The Book of Women's Firsts.* New York: Random House, 1992, pp. 408-09.

1980 ▪ **Marjorie Swank Matthews** (1916-1986), an American Protestant Christian leader, was chosen to become the first woman bishop (a religious official who supervises ministers) in the United Methodist Church. (The Methodist Church, founded by British theologian John Wesley [1703-1791], is a Protestant Christian denomination that stresses individual and social morality.)

Source: *The Christian Century,* August 13, 1980, p. 24.

1982 ▪ **Yvonne Reed Chappelle** (1938-), an American religious leader, was the first African-American woman ordained in the Unitarian Universalist Association. (The Unitarian Universalist Association was formed in 1961 by a merger of the Unitarian and the Universalist churches, Protestant Christian denominations that have similar doctrines. Unitarians believe the deity exists only in one person, as opposed to the traditional Christian belief in the trinity: the father [God], son [Jesus of Nazareth] and the holy spirit. Universalists believe that all human beings will eventually be saved from sin.) Chappelle graduated from the Howard School of Divinity.

Source: *Jet.* February 11, 1982, p. 32.

1985 ▪ **Amy Eilberg** (1954-), an American Jewish religious leader, was the first woman to become a Conservative Jewish rabbi. (Conservative Judaism adheres to the laws of the Torah, the book of Jewish laws, and the Talmud, the authoritative source of Jewish traditions. A rabbi is one who officiates at Jewish religious services.) In 1985 the Rabbinical Assembly of the Conservative movement amended its constitution to allow female rabbis. In May of the same year Eilberg was ordained.

Source: Read, Phyllis J., and Bernard L. Witlieb, *The Book of Women's Firsts.* New York: Random House, 1992, pp. 140-41.

1986 ▪ **Leslie Alexander,** an American Jewish religious leader, became the first female rabbi of a major United States Conservative Jewish synagogue. (Conservative Judaism adheres to the laws of the Torah, the book of Jewish laws, and the Talmud, the authoritative source of Jewish traditions. A rabbi is one who officiates at Jewish religious services.) Alexander presided over the Adat Ari El synagogue in North Hollywood, California, which had a congregation of 850 families.

Source: *Working Woman.* November-December, 1996, p. 76.

1989 ▪ **Barbara Clementine Harris** (1931-), an American religious leader, became the first Episcopal woman bishop. (The Episcopal Church is the American form of the Anglican Church, a Protestant Christian denomination that is the official religion of Great Britain. The Anglican Church is similar to the Roman Catholic Church, except that the pope is not recognized as the ultimate religious authority. A bishop supervises ministers and other clergy.) The appointment of Harris caused a tremendous stir in the Anglican community throughout England and North America. Some male Episcopal clergy claimed they would not recognize her as bishop nor accept priests she ordained. As an African-American woman, however, Harris had a long history of overcoming prejudice and opposition. She ultimately prevailed, and her ordination paved the way for other women. In 1990 Penelope Jamieson (1942-) became the first female Anglican bishop in Great Britain.

Source: Parry, Melanie, ed., *Larousse Dictionary of Women.* New York: Larousse Kingfisher Chambers, Inc., 1995, p. 300.

1992 ▪ **April Ulring Larson,** an American religious leader, was the first woman to be appointed a Lutheran bishop in North America. (The first Protestant Christian denomination, the Lutheran Church was founded by the German theologian Martin Luther [1483-1546]. It is based on the belief that a person's religious commitment is determined by faith in God alone and not by obedience to church authorities.) In 1992 Larson became head of the LaCrosse, Wisconsin, Synod (a regional organization of congregations), which consisted of 40,000 congregation members, 80 churches, and 97 clergy.

Source: *National Catholic Reporter.* October 30, 1992, p. 7.

1995 ▪ **Mary Helen MacKillop** (1842-1909), a Roman Catholic nun, became Australia's first saint. Known as "Mother Mary," MacKillop cofounded—with Father Tenison-Woods—the Society of the Sisters of St. Joseph of the Sacred Heart (a Roman Catholic religious order for women that is called the "Little Joeys") in 1866. The order quickly grew to include 170 schools and 160 convents. As the result of religious rivalries, however, Mother Mary was excommunicated (ejected from the church) in 1871. Reinstated two years later by Pope Pius IX, she continued her work of educating poor children and caring for orphans and unwed mothers. In 1995 MacKillop was declared a saint by Pope John Paul II, who honored her miraculous curing of a woman from leukemia. MacKillop has become a rallying symbol for feminist Australian Catholics.

Source: Parry, Melanie, ed., *Larousse Dictionary of Women.* New York: Larousse Kingfisher Chambers, Inc., 1995, p. 423.

Science and
Technology

Behavioral and Social Science
Natural Science
Physical Science
Technical Science
Space Exploration

Behavioral and Social Science

c. 1890 ▪ **Margaret Murray** (1863-1963), an English archaeologist, was the first woman to conduct her own archaeological digs. (An archaeologist studies the remains of the past, such as fossils, relics, buildings, and monuments.) Also a professor and author, Murray specialized in Egyptology (the study of ancient Egyptian culture) and later wrote extensively about witchcraft in Europe.

Source: Chicago, Judy, *The Dinner Party.* New York: Anchor, 1979, p. 192.

1895 ▪ **Margaret Benson** and **Helen Gourlay,** English archaeologists, led the first all-female team to excavate the Temple of the Goddess Mut at Karnac in Egypt. (An archaeologist studies the remains of the past, such as fossils, relics, buildings, and monuments.) Working as amateur archaeologists, the two English women and their team spent two years at the site, both digging and entertaining the European aristocracy who came to visit the famous temple.

Source: *The Times Literary Supplement.* October 21, 1994, pp. 7-8.

Atmospheric chemist Susan Solomon was the first person to explain the "hole" in the ozone layer. (See "Natural Science" entry dated 1986.)

c. 1900 ▪ **Esther Boise Van Deman** (1862-1937), an American scholar, was the first female Roman field archaeologist. (An archaeologist studies the remains of the past, such as fossils, relics, buildings, and monuments. The field is the site where remains are found.) Educated at Bryn Mawr College and the University of Chicago, Van Deman won a fellowship to the American School of Classical Studies in Rome, Italy, in 1901. After 1906 Van Deman lived and worked in Rome, where she was associated with the American Academy. She had a distinguished career as a field researcher, teacher, and writer.

Source: James, Edward T., and others, eds., *Notable American Women, 1607-1950: A Biographical Dictionary*. Cambridge, Massachusetts: Harvard University Press, 1971, pp. 507-08.

1901 ▪ **Harriet Boyd Howes** (1871-1945), an American archaeologist, was the first person to discover the site of the ancient Minoan town of Gournia, on the island of Crete. (An archaeologist studies the remains of the past, such as fossils, relics, buildings, and monuments.) Howes spent three years excavating (digging out) the area; she later published her findings in a report that is still studied by archaeologists.

Source: James, Edward T., and others, eds., *Notable American Women, 1607-1950: A Biographical Dictionary*. Cambridge, Massachusetts: Harvard University Press, 1971, pp. 160-61.

1902 ▪ **Alice Fletcher** (1838-1923), an American anthropologist, founded the American Anthropological Association. (An anthropologist studies the origins, ethnic distribution, and social and cultural patterns of human beings.) Fletcher was a student of Native North American tribes, working on their behalf in Washington, D.C., and recording their life and rituals in the field. She was also active in the women's liberation movement. In 1904 Fletcher published *The Hako: A Pawnee Ceremony*.

Source: Read, Phyllis J., and Bernard L. Witlieb, *The Book of Women's Firsts*. New York: Random House, 1992, p. 160.

1902 ▪ **Zelia Maria Magdalena Nuttall** (1857-1933), a pioneering American archaeologist, was the first person to establish the historical authenticity of two Mexican codices (ancient books). (An archaeologist studies the remains of the past, such as fossils, relics, buildings, and monuments.) She gave her name to the first of these books, the *Codex Nuttall,* when it was published with her commentary in 1902. Nuttall held the position of special honorary assistant in Mexican archaeology at Harvard's Peabody Museum in Cambridge, Massachusetts, from 1886 until her death. She was the only woman in a group of pioneering archaeologists working in America at the turn of the century.

Source: James, Edward T., and others, eds., *Notable American Women, 1607-1950: A Biographical Dictionary.* Cambridge, Massachusetts: Harvard University Press, 1971, pp. 640-42.

1916 ▪ Leta Stetter Hollingworth (1886-1939), an American educational psychologist, was the first person to submit theories of male superiority to scientific investigation. (An educational psychologist studies how people learn.) She completed her doctoral thesis on this subject at Columbia University in New York City in 1916. Hollingworth went on to a distinguished career in her field and wrote several now-classic books on the development of children and adolescents. She was also the first civil service psychologist in the state of New York. It was reported that when she started at Bellevue Hospital in New York City in 1914 and identified herself as a psychologist, the head of the psychopathic service (treatment of mental disorders) needed an explanation of her new profession.

Source: Parry, Melanie, ed., *Larousse Dictionary of Women.* New York: Larousse Kingfisher Chambers, Inc., 1995, p. 322.

c. 1930 ▪ Ruth Fulton Benedict (1887-1948), an American anthropologist, was the first American woman to become the leader of a learned profession. (An anthropologist studies the origins, ethnic distribution, and social and cultural patterns of human beings.) After earning a degree from Vassar College, Benedict went on to study under famous anthropologist Franz Boas at Columbia University. She received her doctorate in 1923. Benedict first specialized in the study of Native Americans, then in Egyptian and Japanese cultures. As she began to

Working with her husband Louis, English archaeologist Mary Leakey discovered a 1.75-million-year-old skull.

teach at Columbia University in the 1920s, she fostered the careers of American anthropologists Margaret Mead (1901-1978) and later, Zora Neale Hurston (1901-1960; also famous as a fiction writer and autobiographer). Benedict published her famous introductory text, *Patterns of Culture,* in 1934. She served as president of the American Anthropological Association from 1947 until 1948, when she became a full professor at Columbia.

Source: James, Edward T., and others, eds., *Notable American Women, 1607-1950: A Biographical Dictionary.* Cambridge, Massachusetts: Harvard University Press, 1971, pp. 128-31.

c. 1950 ▪ Kathleen Mary Kenyon (1906-1978), an English archaeologist, was the first person successfully to excavate the site of Jericho. (An archaeologist studies the remains of the past, such as fossils, relics, buildings, and monuments.) An ancient city in Palestine, Jericho is mentioned frequently in the Hebrew Bible. Kenyon's achievement is significant because

Jericho was considered the oldest known settlement in the world. Kenyon also excavated at sites in Jerusalem, where she was director of the British School of Archaeology from 1951 to 1966. One of the founders of the Institute of Archaeology in London, England, Kenyon published such works as *Digging Up Jericho* (1958), *Archaeology in the Holy Land* (1956), and *Digging Up Jerusalem* (1974).

Source: Magnusson, Magnus, *Larousse Biographical Dictionary*. Edinburgh: Larousse Kingfisher Chambers, Inc., 1994, p. 821.

1959 ▪ Mary Douglas Leakey (1913-), an English archaeologist, discovered a 1.75-million-year-old skull. (An archaeologist studies the remains of the past, such as fossils, relics, buildings, and monuments.) Working with her husband, anthropologist Louis Leakey, she found the skull in the Olduvai Gorge in Tanganyika (now part of Tanzania). The skull became known as the famous "missing link" in human evolution. This discovery suggested that people had evolved in different branches and approximately a million years earlier than had previously been supposed. After her husband's death in 1972, Leakey took over as director of the Olduvai Gorge excavations, becoming the first woman to hold this position. Through her work she became the leading authority on prehistoric technology and culture.

Source: Parry, Melanie, ed., *Larousse Dictionary of Women*. New York: Larousse Kingfisher Chambers, Inc., 1995, p. 388.

Jane Goodall, an English zoologist, was the first person to conduct long-term studies of chimpanzees in their natural habitat.

1960 ▪ Jane Goodall (1934-), an English zoologist, was the first person to conduct long-term studies of chimpanzees in their natural habitat. (A zoologist studies animal life.) She began her work at Gombe Stream on the shores of Lake Tanganyika in Tanzania in 1960, and reported on her study six years later. Goodall's findings were significant because she

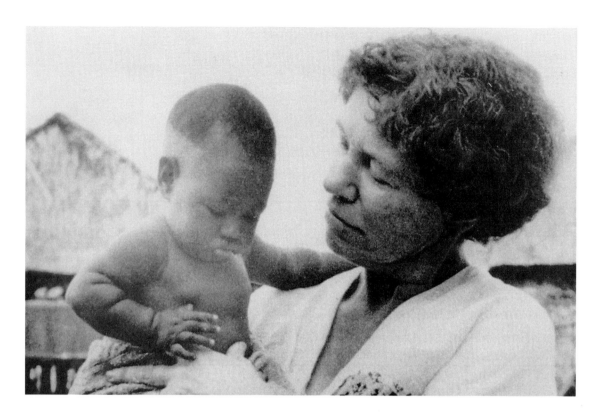

Anthropologist Margaret Mead (pictured here with Manus children in 1928) theorized about the ways culture influences the development of personality.

demonstrated that chimpanzees are highly intelligent social animals. Continuing her research at Gombe Stream, Goodall published books on wild dogs, jackals, and hyenas as well as chimpanzees.

Source: Parry, Melanie, ed., *Larousse Dictionary of Women.* New York: Larousse Kingfisher Chambers, Inc., 1995, p. 275.

1967 ▪ Dian Fossey (1932-1985), an English primatologist, was the first woman to work successfully with gorillas in the African wild. (A primatologist studies monkeys, chimpanzees, and gorillas). Beginning her study under the sponsorship of archaeologist Louis Leakey, Fossey moved to Rwanda and founded the Karisoke Research Center in 1967. Her interests shifted from observation of gorillas to their preservation. Fossey wrote about her experiences in *Gorillas in the Mist* (1983), which became the basis for a feature film starring Sigourney Weaver. Fossey was found dead at her camp under mysterious circumstances in 1985; many people believed she was murdered by a poacher angered at her efforts to stop the killing of gorillas.

Source: Brockman, Norbert, *An African Biographical Dictionary*. Santa Barbara: ABC-Clio, 1994, p. 119.

1976 ▪ **Margaret Mead** (1901-1978), an American anthropologist, was the first woman to have a chair named after her at the American Museum of Natural History in New York City. (An anthropologist studies the origins, ethnic distribution, and social and cultural patterns of human beings.) She was influenced by Columbia University anthropologist Ruth Benedict (1887-1948) to pursue a career in anthropology. While a student at Barnard College, Mead received her first grant to study in Samoa. In 1926, she was appointed assistant curator of ethnology (the study of culture according to race) at the American Museum of Natural History. As her career in anthropology progressed, she undertook expeditions to Samoa and New Guinea. Mead wrote about her observations in these two countries in *Coming of Age in Samoa* (1928) and *Growing up in New Guinea* (1930). She later theorized about the ways culture influenced the development of personality in such works as *Male and Female* (1949) and *Growth and Culture* (1941).

Source: Magnusson, Magnus, *Larousse Biographical Dictionary*. Edinburgh: Larousse Kingfisher Chambers, Inc., 1994, p. 996.

Natural Science

1675 ▪ **Maria Sibylla Merian** (1647-1717) was the first German woman to become a scientific illustrator. Merian traveled widely in Europe and in the East and West Indies. Although she published several books detailing flowers and insects, she died in poverty. In 1997 the U.S. Postal Service featured two of Merian's drawings on postage stamps. These images came from her studies and paintings of insects, birds, and plants during an expedition to Surinam in 1699. Merian's illustrations are exhibited in The National Museum of Women in the Arts in Washington, D. C.

Source: Uglow, Jennifer S., ed., *The Continuum Dictionary of Women's Biography*. New York: Continuum, 1989, pp. 374-75.

Mantell Found Tooth

Mary Anne Mantell was the first person to discover a dinosaur when she found a strange tooth in Cuckfield Quarry in Sussex, England, in 1820.

1744 ▪ **Eliza Lucas Pinckney** (1723-1793), an American agricultural pioneer, was the first woman to cultivate indigo (a plant that yields a dark blue dye), on her plantation near Charleston, South Carolina. Carefully researching various crops— especially those that flourished in the West Indies—she also experimented with flax, hemp, and silk, establishing a successful plantation and lucrative trade with England. A dress made from her silk was given to the Princess of Wales in England.

Source: Ravenel, Harriet Horry Rutledge, *Eliza Pinckney.* New York: Scribner's, 1896.

1757 ▪ **Jane Colden** (1722-1764), an American scientific illustrator, discovered and named a new species of gardenia. She was the daughter of Cadwallader Colden, who served as acting British governor in the New York colony. Trained in botany by her father, Colden catalogued and illustrated more than three hundred specimens of plants in the New York region by 1757. She did not label the plants with their Latin names, however, because her father did not teach her the language, thinking women were incapable of learning it. In 1770, four years after Colden died in childbirth, the British Royal Society published a description of a gardenia species and attributed its discovery to naturalist Alexander Garden. Colden, in fact, had discovered and named the plant.

Source: Trager, James, *The Women's Chronology.* New York: Holt, 1991, p. 192.

1824 ▪ **Mary Anning** (1799-1847) was the first person to discover a plesiosaurus (any of a suborder of Mesozoic marine reptiles; Anning found an almost perfect fossil of this creature in Dorset, England). Anning's first major discovery was made in 1811 when she discovered the fossil skeleton of an ichthyosaurus (any of an order of extinct Mesozoic reptiles), which was later displayed in the British Museum of Natural History. In 1828 she discovered the first skeleton of a pterodactyl (a flying dinosaur with a large wingspan).

Source: Ogilvie, Marilyn Bailey, *Women in Science: Antiquity through the Nineteenth Century.* Cambridge, Massachusetts: M.I.T. Press, 1986, p. 31.

1883 ▪ **Marianne North** (1830-1890), an English botanical painter (a person who paints flowers and plants), discovered an unknown capuchin tree. North traveled extensively painting flowers. In 1880, at the suggestion of famous naturalist Charles Darwin (1809-1882), North went to Australia to improve her collection. While in the Seychelles (a group of islands off Tanzania in the Indian Ocean) in 1883, North discovered a capuchin tree that was later named *Northia seychellana* in her honor.

Source: Parry, Melanie, ed., *Larousse Dictionary of Women.* New York: Larousse Kingfisher Chambers, Inc,. 1995, p. 498.

1894 ▪ **Florence Bascom** (1862-1945), an American geologist (a scientist who studies rocks and minerals), was the first woman to be elected a fellow of the Geological Society of America; Bascom was subsequently the first woman to serve as its vice president. She was also the first woman to receive an appointment to the U.S. Geological Survey. In addition to her firsts in the field of geology, Bascom became the first woman to earn a doctorate from Johns Hopkins University in Baltimore, Maryland in 1893. She taught geology at Bryn Mawr College in Pennsylvania for most of her career.

Source: Bailey, Brooke, *The Remarkable Live of 100 Women Healers and Scientists.* Holbrook, Massachusetts: Bob Adams, 1994, pp. 14-15.

1909 ▪ **Annie Montague Alexander** (1867-1949), an American naturalist, established the first natural history museum on the west coast of the United States, in Berkeley, California. Naturalist Joseph Grinnell was her collaborator and served as the museum's first director. Alexander also established the department of paleontology (the study of fossils) at the University of California at Berkeley in the same year. Alexander devoted her life to this field and to the sciences of botany (the study of plants), ornithology (the study of birds), and mammology (the study of mammals).

Source: Bailey, Brooke, *The Remarkable Lives of 100 Women Healers and Scientists.* Holbrook, Massachusetts: Bob Adams, 1994, pp. 4-5.

1929 ▪ **Florence Merriam Bailey** (1863-1948), an American ornithologist, became the first female fellow of the American Ornithologists' Union (AOU). (An ornithologist studies birds.) Founder of one of America's first Audubon Society chapters (an organization started by John James Audubon [1785- 1851] for the study of birds), Bailey was widely recognized for her lifelong interest in birds. In 1885 she was the first woman to become an associate member of the AOU. In 1931 she won the Union's prestigious Bruster Medal, becoming the first woman to receive this award. Among Bailey's publications is *Birds of New Mexico* (1928).

Source: Ogilvie, Marilyn Bailey, *Women in Science: Antiquity through the Nineteenth Century*. Cambridge, Massachusetts: M.I.T. Press, 1986, pp. 34-35.

1930 ▪ **Caroline Dormon** (1888-1971) was one of the first three women to be elected to associate membership in the Society of American Foresters. Dormon established her career as a naturalist (a person who studies natural life) and conservationist (someone who works to preserve nature) in her native Louisiana.

Source: Bailey, Brooke, *The Remarkable Lives of 100 Women Healers and Scientists*. Holbrook, Massachusetts: Bob Adams, 1994, pp. 54-55.

1936 ▪ **Inge Lehmann** (1888-1993), a Danish seismologist, discovered the earth's solid core. Originally trained as a mathematician, Lehmann eventually turned her attention to seismology (the study of earthquakes). After earning a master's degree in geodesy (a branch of mathematics concerned with determining the exact size and shape of the Earth) from the University of Copenhagen in 1928, Lehmann was named chief of the Royal Danish Geodetic Institute. In 1936 she published her most significant finding, the discovery of the earth's inner core, under the simple title "P." (The letter P stood for three types of waves generated by Pacific earthquakes that Lehmann had been observing throughout the planet for ten years.) In 1971 Lehmann was awarded the William Bowie Medal of the American Geophysical Union.

Source: *Current Biography Yearbook: 1962*. New York: Wilson, 1963, pp. 250-52.

1938 ▪ **Margaret Morse Nice** (1883-1974), an American ornithologist, became the first woman to serve as head of a major ornithological society in the United States when she was elected president of the Wilson Ornithological Society. (An ornithologist studies birds.) While living in Columbus, Ohio, Nice began studying the territorial behavior of birds. She placed colored bands on the birds' legs and observed their movements for years in a way no one had before. With the publication of her two-part *Studies in the Life History of the Song Sparrow* in 1937 and 1943, Nice became one of the world's leading ornithologists. In 1969 the Wilson Ornithological Society inaugurated a grant in Nice's name to be awarded to self-trained amateur bird researchers.

Source: Conway, Jill K., *Written by Herself.* New York: Vintage Books, 1991.

1948 ▪ **Tilly Edinger** (1897-1967), a German-born American paleontologist, proposed a new theory of evolution. (A paleobiologist studies animal fossils.) After earning a doctorate in natural philosophy from the University of Frankfurt in 1921, Edinger was the curator (director) of fossil vertebrates (animals with spinal cords) at the Senckenberg Museum in Frankfurt. After fleeing the Nazis, Edinger became a researcher at the Museum of Comparative Zoology at Harvard University in 1940. In 1948 she published *Evolution of the Horse Brain,* which established that the rate of evolution varies for different species. She challenged the commonly held notion that evolution consisted of a progression from "lower" animals, such as rats and mice, up to the "highest" creatures, human beings. She showed that evolution is actually a complex branching process. Edinger is credited as one of the originators of paleoneurology (the study of the brain through fossil remains).

Source: Sicherman, Barbara, and Carol H. Green, eds., *Notable American Women: The Modern Period.* Cambridge, Massachusetts: Harvard University Press, pp. 218-19.

c. 1950s ▪ **Ruth Patrick** (1907-), an American limnologist, was the first woman to head the Academy of Natural Sciences. (A limnologist studies freshwater biology.) After earning a doctorate from the University of Virginia, Patrick advanced the

Limnologist Ruth Patrick was the first woman to head the Academy of Natural Sciences.

field of ecology (the study of organisms within their environment). Her studies of diatoms (microscopic species of algae) in rivers around the world have provided methods for monitoring water pollution. She has also demonstrated how to maintain a desired balance of different forms of algae in water. Patrick is perhaps best known for the invention of the diatometer, a device that measures pollution in fresh water. In 1975 she received the prestigious Tyler Ecology Award for her studies of freshwater ecosystems.

Source: Vare, Ethlie Ann, and Greg Ptacek, *Mothers of Invention: From the Bra to the Bomb, Forgotten Women and Their Unforgettable Ideas.* New York: William Morrow, 1988, pp. 179-80.

1952 ▪ **Marie Tharp** (1920-), an American oceanic cartographer, codiscovered the valley that divides the Mid-Atlantic Ridge. (An oceanic cartographer is someone who makes maps of the ocean floor.) After earning a master's degree in geology from the University of Michigan in 1944, Tharp worked as a research assistant at Columbia University. With fellow researcher Bruce Heezen, she started mapping the entire ocean floor. When the duo found the Mid-Atlantic Ridge, geologists were able to determine "sea floor spreading," the creation of the sea floor at ridges that rippled outward. This discovery led to the eventual acceptance of the theory of continental drift, now called plate tectonics. In 1977, shortly before Heezen's death, Tharp and Heezen published the *World Ocean Floor Panorama*. In 1978 both researchers received the Hubbard Medal of the National Geographic Society.

Source: "Mappers of the Deep," *Natural History,* October, 1986, pp. 49-62.

1958 ▪ **Florence W. van Straten** (1913-), an American meteorologist, originated cloud seeding. (A meteorologist studies and forecasts weather.) After earning a Ph.D. from New York University and serving in the WAVES (a women's naval corps), van Straten became director of the Technical Requirements

Branch of the U.S. Naval Weather Service. During World War II (1939-1945) she began conducting research on how to control and modify the weather to stop a hurricane or end rain in flooded areas. While working for the Weather Service, van Straten developed the theory that rain is dependent upon evaporation rates within a cloud. In 1958 she successfully demonstrated a method for creating or dissipating (decreasing in size) clouds by "seeding" them with a material that could change temperatures by absorbing light.

Source: McMurray, Emily J., ed., *Notable Twentieth- Century Scientists*. Detroit: Gale Research, 1995, pp. 2080- 81.

1962 ▪ Joy (Friederike Gessner) Adamson (1910-1980), an Austrian naturalist, started the World Wildlife Fund. Her career as a professional conservationist began in 1956 when her husband, George Adamson, shot a lioness that had attacked him. After the animal's death, George brought the lioness's three cubs home. Joy wanted to take care of all three of them, but George sent two cubs to a zoo. Naming the third cub Elsa, Joy Adamson tried to raise her so she could return to the wild. After a failed attempt, Elsa was able to join a pride (family of lions), mate, and have six cubs. Adamson's experiences with Elsa led her to found the World Wildlife Fund in the United States in 1962. Adamson was perhaps best known, however, for her books about Elsa, among them *Born Free* (1960), which became the basis for a feature film. Adamson was murdered in her home in Kenya in 1980.

Source: Parry, Melanie, ed., *Larousse Dictionary of Women*. New York: Larousse Kingfisher Chambers, Inc,. 1995, p. 5.

1962 ▪ Rachel Louise Carson (1907-1964), an American marine biologist, was the first person to focus public attention on the danger of pesticides (chemicals used to destroy pests). Carson became best known as a naturalist (a person who studies organisms in nature) with the publication of *The Sea*

Marine biologist Rachel Carson helped launch the ecology movement with books like Silent Spring.

Around Us (1951), and her powerful 1962 work, *Silent Spring,* which exposed the consequences of America's use of environmental pollutants. Carson testified before the U.S. Senate on the effects of marine pollution on the ocean's food chain. Largely on the strength of Carson's testimony, controls were placed on pollution. Carson was one of the scientists who helped launch the ecology movement (an organized effort to maintain the balance of nature).

Source: Bailey, Brook, *The Remarkable Lives of 100 Women Healers and Scientists.* Holbrook, Massachusetts: Bob Adams, 1994, pp. 40-41.

1963 ▪ Margaret B. Davis (1931-), an American paleoecologist, developed a new theory of ancient life. (A paleoecologist studies fossils and their environment.) After completing a doctorate in biology at Harvard University in 1957, she pursued research in the new field of palynology (the study of pollen and spores). In 1963 Davis attracted international attention with a paper on the theory of pollen analysis published in the *American Journal of Science.* Davis challenged the prevailing scientific idea that plant and animal communities tend to be stable, moving unchanged to new locations as the climate changes. By studying pollen from ancient plants she reconstructed past plant communities and showed how they change in response to variations in climate or other environmental influences. Davis concluded that plant and animal communities changed more rapidly than scientists had assumed, thus opening the door to a new scientific method of understanding the history and ecology of plants (interrelationship between plants and their environment).

Source: *Bulletin of the Ecological Society of America.* September, 1987, pp. 490-91.

1986 ▪ Susan Solomon (1956-), an American atmospheric chemist, was the first person to explain the "hole" in the ozone layer. (An atmospheric chemist studies the action of chemicals in the Earth's atmosphere.) After earning a Ph.D. in chemistry from the Illinois Institute of Technology in 1981, Solomon became a researcher at the National Oceanic and Atmospheric Administration Aeronomy Laboratory in Boulder, Colorado. In

1985 scientists reported that, during the spring months in the Southern Hemisphere (September to October), the density of the ozone layer (the layer of the atmosphere containing ozone, a form of oxygen that blocks solar radiation) over Antarctica was decreasing rapidly. The following year, in an effort to find the cause of this "hole," the scientific community planned an expedition to Antarctica to measure atmospheric levels of ozone and nitrogen dioxide (a gas that causes rust). Solomon volunteered to head the project. Upon her return to Colorado, she reported that chloroflurocarbons (a mixture of carbon, chlorine, fluorine, and sometimes hydrogen) caused the ozone hole. Chloroflurocarbons, she said, were released into the atmosphere by leaking refrigeration equipment, foams, or other substances. Solomon's explanation is now generally accepted by scientists, and has led many countries of the world to curtail the production and use of chloroflurocarbons.

Source: Glanz, James, "How Susan Solomon's Research Changed Our View of the Earth," *R & D.* September, 1992, p. 46.

Physical Science

First century ▪ Maria the Jewess, a first-century Alexandrian alchemist, is known as one of the founders of the science of chemistry and the first woman to work as a modern chemist. In addition to her chemical studies, Maria invented laboratory equipment that remained in use for centuries, including the double boiler, used to maintain substances at a constant temperature (a device still known today as a "bain-marie").

Source: Uglow, Jennifer S., ed., *The Continuum Dictionary of Women's Biography.* New York: Continuum, 1989, p. 356.

Late 1700s ▪ Maria Gaetana Agnesi (1718-1799) was the first woman admitted to the Bologna Academy of Sciences. Agnesi was honored for her achievements in mathematics, science, and philosophy, for which she drew on her extensive knowledge of several languages.

Source: Ogilvie, Marilyn Bailey, *Women in Science: Antiquity through the Nineteenth Century.* Cambridge, Massachusetts: M.I.T. Press, 1986, pp. 26-28.

Queen Built Observatory

Sonduk, a Korean queen, built the first observatory in the Far East. Daughter of the king of the Silla dynasty, Sonduk ruled for fifteen years. During her reign she built Ch'omsong-dae ("Tower of the Moon and Stars"), the first known observatory (a building designed for observing the sky and stars) in the Far East (the countries of eastern and southeastern Asia). The Ch'omsong-dae has remained standing through the twentieth century.

1805 ▪ **Jane Marcet** (1769-1858) was the first English writer to direct her written work on scientific subjects specifically toward women. In 1805 Marcet published her very popular *Conversations on Chemistry: Intended More Specifically for the Female Sex,* which went through 16 British and 15 American editions.

Source: Uglow, Jennifer S., ed., *The Continuum Dictionary of Women's Biography.* New York: Continuum, 1989, p. 354.

1835 ▪ **Mary Fairfax Greig Somerville** (1780-1872), a Scottish mathematician and astronomer, and **Caroline Herschel** (1750-1872), a German astronomer, were the first women to become honorary members of the Royal Astronomical Society in England. (An astronomer studies stars and other celestial bodies.) Herschel was honored for her work in astronomy and her discovery of comets. Somerville was recognized for her writing on a range of scientific subjects. Somerville also gave her name to one of the first two women's colleges at Oxford University.

Source: Ogilvie, Marilyn Bailey, *Women in Science: Antiquity through the Nineteenth Century.* Cambridge, Massachusetts: M.I.T. Press, 1986, pp. 161-66.

1847 ▪ **Maria Mitchell** (1818-1889), an American astronomer, was the first woman in the United States to discover a comet. (An astronomer studies stars and other celestial bodies.) The comet was later named for her. Regarded as one of the first women astronomers, Mitchell made her discovery at Nantucket, Massachusetts. In 1848 she was also the first—and until 1943, the only—woman elected to the American Academy of Arts and Sciences. (The Academy honored her for her discovery of the comet.) In 1873 Mitchell was founder of the Association of the Advancement of Women, as well as vice-president of the American Social Science Association.

Source: Ogilvie, Marilyn Bailey, *Women in Science: Antiquity through the Nineteenth Century.* Cambridge, Massachusetts: M.I.T. Press, 1986, pp. 133-39.

Late 1800s ▪ Dorothea Klumpke (1861-1942), an American astronomer, was the first woman elected to the Astronomical Society in France, in the late nineteenth century. (An astronomer studies stars and other celestial bodies.) Klumpke was recognized for a distinguished career in astronomy in which she achieved a number of firsts. She was the first woman allowed to work at the Paris Observatoire and the first woman to earn a doctorate in mathematics at that institution.

Source: Uglow, Jennifer S., ed., *The Continuum Dictionary of Women's Biography.* New York: Continuum, 1989, p. 301.

1889 ▪ Antonia Maury (1866-1952), an American astronomer, was the first woman to discover two double stars. (An astronomer studies stars and other celestial bodies.) Known as a binary, a double star is a pair of stars revolving around a common center of gravity. Maury determined the period of the spectral lines (length of the radiation spectrum) of the stars Mizar and Beta Aurigae while doing research at the Harvard Observatory.

Source: Uglow, Jennifer S., ed., *The Continuum Dictionary of Women's Biography.* New York: Continuum, 1989, p. 366.

Logician Christine Ladd-Franklin claimed that color vision evolved from light sensitivity.

1892 ▪ Christine Ladd-Franklin (1847-1930), an American logician, introduced her controversial color theory. Ladd-Franklin was born in Windsor, Connecticut. After earning a Ph.D. in logic and mathematics at Johns Hopkins University in 1883, she turned to the study of vision. She presented her own color theory to the International Congress of Psychology in London in 1892. In her presentation, Ladd-Franklin claimed that color vision evolves from light (white) sensitivity, as well as the perception of three basic colors, red, green and blue. After a period of controversy, Ladd-Franklin's ideas were accepted by psychologists for many years.

Source: Ogilvie, Marilyn Bailey, *Women in Science: Antiquity through the Nineteenth Century.* Cambridge, Massachusetts: M.I.T. Press, 1986, pp. 116-17.

1894 ▪ **Anna Wessels Williams** (1863-1954), an American bacteriologist, discovered the diphtheria bacillus. (A bacteriologist studies bacteria, or organisms that cause disease.) Williams earned a medical degree in 1891 from the Women's Medical College of the New York Infirmary. In 1894 she volunteered to serve in the bacteriology laboratory at the New York Department of Health, the nation's first city-operated diagnostic laboratory. She began searching for an antitoxin (an antitoxin is a protein produced in the body as a defense against some bacteria) for diphtheria (an inflammation of the heart and nervous system), at the time a leading cause of death among children. Williams's discovery of the *Corynebacterium diphtheria* bacillus (a disease-producing bacterium) led to the development of a diphtheria antitoxin. The antitoxin was soon in use throughout North America and Great Britain.

Source: Sicherman, Barbara, and Carol Hurd Green, eds., *Notable American Women: The Modern Period.* Cambridge, Massachusetts: Belknap Press, 1980, pp. 737-39.

c. 1900 ▪ **Henrietta Swan Leavitt** (1868-1921), an American astronomer, was the first person to discover 2,400 variable stars. (An astronomer studies stars and other celestial bodies.) After graduating from Radcliffe College, where she developed an interest in astronomy, Leavitt became a volunteer at the Harvard College Observatory in Cambridge, Massachusetts. After joining the observatory staff in 1902, Leavitt quickly became the first female head of photographic photometry (a branch of science that deals with measurement of the intensity of light). By 1912 she had successfully demonstrated that there was a relationship between the brightness of stars and the period of their light variation. While studying the constellation Cepheid, Leavitt observed that the apparent magnitude of a star's light and its relative distance from the earth could be calculated according to a mathematical formula. This discovery was significant in making it possible to calculate the distances of stars and led to further investigations of the Milky Way galaxy (the galaxy of which our solar system is part).

Source: Magnusson, Magnus, *Larousse Biographical Dictionary.* Edinburgh: Larousse Kingfisher Chambers, Inc., 1994, p. 872.

c. 1902 ▪ **Dorothy Reed Mendenhall** (1874-1964), an American pathologist (a scientist who studies diseases), discovered that Hodgkin's disease was not a form of tuberculosis. (Hodgkin's disease causes inflammation of lymph nodes and other organs as well as anemia, or deficiency of iron in the blood. Tuberculosis is caused by bacteria, or disease-causing organisms, in the lungs.) In 1900 Mendenhall was one of the first women to graduate from Johns Hopkins with a medical degree. The next year she received a fellowship in pathology, which led to her discovery of the nature of Hodgkin's disease. As a result of her work, the cell type characteristic of Hodgkin's disease bears her name.

In 1906 Mendenhall married Charles Elwood Mendenhall and began to raise a family. The loss of her first child due to poor obstetrics (the treatment of a woman during pregnancy and after childbirth) changed her research career to a lifelong effort to reduce infant death rates. Mendenhall was successful in bringing about the establishment of weight and height standards for children from birth to age six, and she initiated programs that stressed the health of both the mother and child in the birthing process.

Source: Read, Phyllis J., and Bernard L. Witlieb, *The Book of Women's Firsts.* New York: Random House, 1992, pp. 362-63.

1902 ▪ **Ida Henrietta Hyde** (1857-1945), an American marine physiologist, was the first woman elected to membership in the American Physiological Society. (A marine physiologist studies animals that live in oceans and seas.) In 1896 she was the first woman to receive a doctoral degree from the University of Heidelberg in Germany. Hyde had a distinguished career in marine physiology, conducting much of her research at the Woods Hole Oceanographic Institute in Massachusetts. Hyde was also the first woman to do research at Harvard Medical School. During her work on the physiology of both vertebrates (animals with spines) and invertebrates (animals without spines), she pioneered the use of micro-electrode techniques. (A micro-electrode is a tiny device that is inserted into a living biological cell or tissue to study its electrical characteristics.)

Source: James, Edward T., and others, eds., *Notable American Women, 1607-1950: A Biographical Dictionary.* Cambridge, Massachusetts: Harvard University Press, 1971, pp. 247-49.

Researcher Marie Curie was the first person to win two Nobel prizes.

1903 ▪ Nettie Maria Stevens (1861-1912), an American biologist, was one of the first scientists to demonstrate that sex is determined by a particular chromosome. Stevens conducted her research at Bryn Mawr College in Pennsylvania, where she was a professor of biology from 1903 until her death.

Source: Ogilvie, Marilyn Bailey, *Women in Science: Antiquity through the Nineteenth Century.* Cambridge, Massachusetts: M.I.T. Press, 1986, pp. 167-69.

1903 ▪ Marie Curie (1867-1934) was the first woman to win a Nobel Prize when she won the award in physics (an honor she shared with her husband Pierre [1859-1906] and Antoine Henri Becquerel [1852-1908], a colleague at the Sorbonne in Paris). The prize was awarded for the group's discovery of radioactivity (the property possessed by some elements of spontaneously emitting energy particles). When Pierre Curie died in a traffic accident, Marie was appointed to fill his chair as professor of physics at the Sorbonne, becoming the first woman in France to reach professorial rank. Marie Curie was also the first person to win two Nobel prizes when she was awarded the prize for chemistry in 1911, an honor she earned for the isolation of pure radium.

Source: Sanders, Dennis, *The First of Everything.* New York: Delacorte Press, 1981, p. 166.

1907 ▪ Mary Engle Pennington (1872-1952), an American chemist, was the first woman to work as a bacteriological chemist for the newly created U.S. Department of Agriculture (USDA). (A bacteriological chemist studies the chemical activity of bacteria, or disease-causing organisms.) Pennington passed the civil service exam in 1907 under the name M.E. Pennington. Unaware that Pennington was a woman, the government gave her a post as bacteriological chemist. She was promoted to head of the food research lab in 1908. During Pennington's tenure the laboratory changed procedures in the warehousing, packaging, and refrigeration of food during transport. Pennington was the recipient of several awards, including the Garvan Medal from the American Chemical Society in 1940.

Source: Sicherman, Barbara, and Carol Hurd Green, eds., *Notable American Women: The Modern Period.* Cambridge, Massachusetts: Belknap Press, 1980.

1910 ▪ Williamina Stevens Fleming (1857-1911), a Scottish-born American astronomer, was the first person to discover "white dwarfs," hot, extremely dense and compact stars in their final evolutionary stage. Fleming published her discovery in 1910. In 1906 she was also the first woman to be appointed to the Royal Astronomical Society in Greenwich, England; she was also the first woman to serve as curator (head administrator) of astronomical photographs at Harvard University, a post she assumed in 1898.

Source: James, Edward T., and others, eds., *Notable American Women, 1607-1950: A Biographical Dictionary.* Cambridge, Massachusetts: Harvard University Press, 1971, pp. 628-30.

1913 ▪ Marguerite Davis (1887-1967), an American chemist, codiscovered vitamins A and B. Davis was born in Racine, Wisconsin. She received a bachelor of science degree from the University of California at Berkeley in 1910, then enrolled at the University of Wisconsin for graduate studies. During her time at Wisconsin, Davis began her work with Elmer Verner McCollum (1879-1967), who had been studying nutrition for several years. In 1913 Davis and McCollum discovered a factor in some fats that apparently was essential to life. Because the substance differed chemically from one described earlier by other scientists, the duo named theirs "A." They gave the name "B" to the other substance, which was water soluble. The identification of A and B led later to the discovery of the other vitamins and their specific roles in nutrition, as well as which foods contain them.

Source: McMurray, Emily J., ed., *Notable Twentieth-Century Scientists.* Detroit: Gale Research, 1995, pp. 462-63.

c. 1920s ▪ Geraldine Thiele, an American scientist, was the first person to invent an injectable drug to cure shin splints (an often crippling leg ailment) in horses. She also invented a mouthwash for horses that helped to prevent tooth decay and a horse feed that kept manure from smelling offensive.

Source: Vare, Ethlie, and Greg Ptacek, *Mothers of Invention: From the Bra to the Bomb, Forgotten Women and Their Unforgettable Ideas.* New York: William Morrow, 1988, p. 117.

1920 ▪ **Louise Pearce** (1885-1959), an American physician, discovered tryparsamide. The drug was used to conquer African sleeping sickness in the Congo, a colony of Belgium at the time. Pearce was honored for her research with the Order of the Crown of Belgium in 1920, the King Leopold II Prize in 1950, and the Royal Order of the Lion.

Source: Levin, Beatrice, *Women and Medicine: Pioneers Meeting the Challenge!* Lincoln, Nebraska: Media Publishing, 1988, p. 158.

1922 ▪ **Katharine Scott Bishop** (1889-1975), an American physician, codiscovered vitamin E. After receiving a medical degree from Johns Hopkins Medical School in 1915, Scott moved to the University of California Medical School where she was on the faculty and worked with Herbert McLean Evans. In 1922 Bishop and Evans were codiscoverers of vitamin E. The duo proved its existence by identifying its deficiency in laboratory rats. Initially calling what they discovered "substance X," Bishop and Evans observed that depriving rats of the substance disturbed the animals' ability to reproduce. Pure vitamin E was isolated by Evans and others in 1935.

Source: McMurray, Emily J., ed., *Notable Twentieth-Century Scientists.* Detroit: Gale Research, 1995, p. 179.

1923 ▪ **Gladys Rowena Henry Dick** (1881-1963), an American microbiologist, discovered the bacteria that causes scarlet fever. (Scarlet fever is an inflammation of the nose, throat, and mouth accompanied by a red rash. It is caused by streptococci bacteria.) Dick made her discovery while working with her husband, George Francis Dick, at the University of Chicago. The two also developed the skin test, known as the "Dick test," that indicates susceptibility to the disease.

Source: Bailey, Brooke, *The Remarkable Lives of 100 Woman Healers and Scientists.* Holbrook, Massachusetts: Bob Adams, 1994, pp. 52-53.

1925 ▪ Florence Rena Sabin (1871-1953),

an American physician, was the first female member of the National Academy of Sciences. Sabin was honored for her medical research in the field of histology (microscopic study of tissues), during which she determined the origin of red corpuscles (living cells). Sabin was associated with Johns Hopkins University for twenty-five years. She became the school's first female faculty member in 1902, and in 1917 became Johns Hopkins's first female full professor. From 1924-1926, Sabin served as the first female president of the American Association of Anatomists. She was also the first woman elected to the New York Academy of Sciences and the first female member of the Rockefeller Institute.

Physician Flora Rena Sabin served as the first female president of the American Association of Anatomists.

Source: Haber, Louis, *Women Pioneers of Science.* New York: Harcourt Brace Jovanovich, 1979, pp. 30-40.

1928 ▪ Alice Evans (1881-1975), an American microbiolo-

gist, became the first female president of the Society of American Bacteriologists. This organization, now the American Society for Microbiology, promotes education in microbiology (the scientific study of microscopic forms of life) and encourages professional and ethical standards. Evans is best known for discovering that brucellosis (a disease in cattle) and human Malta fever resulted from the same bacterium (disease-causing organism). Although her theory was originally discounted, Evans was eventually instrumental in making the pasteurization of milk a U.S. government requirement.

Source: Parry, Melanie, ed., *Larousse Dictionary of Women.* New York: Larousse Kingfisher Chambers, Inc., 1995, p. 224.

c. 1929 ▪ Tettje Clasina Clay-Jolles (1881-1972), a Dutch

physicist and one of the first women scientists in the Nether-

Physicist Lise Meitner was the first woman to win the Enrico Fermi Award from the Atomic Energy Commission.

lands, codiscovered the relationship between ultraviolet penetration and the ozone layer. From 1920 to 1929, she worked with her husband, Jacob Clay-Jolles, on measuring the intensity of atmospheric radiation. (Atmospheric radiation is electromagnetic waves released into the area above the Earth.) The two researchers discovered that ultraviolet penetration (electromagnetic waves released into the atmosphere) at various latitudes relates directly to the relation between the upper atmosphere and the ozone layer. (The ozone layer is a region in the atmosphere that blocks certain solar rays.)

Source: McMurray, Emily J., ed., *Notable Twentieth-Century Scientists.* Detroit: Gale Research, 1995, pp. 366-67.

c. 1930s ▪ Gladys Anderson Emerson (1903-1984) was the first person to isolate vitamin E. She performed experiments in Berkeley, California, in the 1930s and isolated this vitamin in its pure crystalline form from wheat germ oil.

Source: Uglow, Jennifer S., ed., *The Continuum Dictionary of Women's Biography.* New York: Continuum, 1989, p. 191.

c. 1930s ▪ Lise Meitner (1878-1968), an Austrian physicist, was the first person to use the term "nuclear fission" in reference to the splitting of the atom. This term grew out of her work in nuclear physics with Otto Hahn (1879-1968) at the University of Berlin where she was a research assistant. Meitner and Hahn continued to collaborate for over 30 years in laboratories in Germany, Austria, Denmark, and Sweden. She worked on her own in both the United States and England. In 1966, when the U.S. Atomic Energy Commission gave its Enrico Fermi Award to the team of researchers with whom Meitner had collaborated, she became the first woman to receive this award.

Source: Haber, Louis, *Women Pioneers of Science.* New York: Harcourt Brace Jovanovich, 1979, pp. 41-51.

1931 ▪ Barbara McClintock (1902-1992) was the first female doctoral student at the California Institute of Technology. She went on to become the first female president of the Genetics Society of America, in 1944. McClintock won the Nobel Prize for medicine and physiology on October 10, 1983, receiving recognition for her achievement in discovering the genetic nature of cross fertilization in corn. Her work had far-reaching implications for the study of genetics in both plants and animals.

Source: Levin, Beatrice, *Women and Medicine: Pioneers Meeting the Challenge!* Lincoln, Nebraska: Media Publishing, 1988, pp. 177-80.

1934 ▪ Irène Joliot-Curie (1897-1956), a French biochemist, codiscovered artificial radioactivity. (A biochemist studies chemical compounds in living organisms.) Working with her husband, Frédérick Joliot-Curie (1900-1958), she bombarded aluminum with alpha particles to produce a radioactive isotope. (An alpha particle is a molecule in an organism that is the closest in structure to a group of atoms. A radioactive isotope is one of two or more atoms that have the same number of protons but a different number of neutrons.) The Joliot-Curies were honored for this achievement with the Nobel Prize for chemistry in 1935. Irène Joliot-Curie was the daughter of Nobel-winners Marie and Pierre Curie.

Source: Parry, Melanie, ed., *Larousse Dictionary of Women.* New York: Larousse Kingfisher Chambers, Inc., 1995. p. 350.

1934 ▪ Ida Eva Noddack (1896-), a German chemist, was the first woman to suggest the possibility of nuclear fission in the bombardment of radium when Enrico Fermi first reported his experiments in 1934. Her idea was initially ignored, but credited five years later. Noddack (working with her husband Walter Karl Friedrich Noddack) was also the first woman to discover the missing elements technetium (formerly known as masurium) and rhenium, numbers 43 and 75 on the periodic table, respectively. The latter was named rhenium after the Rhine River near which Noddack was born.

Source: Uglow, Jennifer S., ed., *The Continuum Dictionary of Women's Biography.* New York: Continuum, 1989, p. 404.

1935 ▪ **Dorothy Hansine Andersen** (1901-1963), an American pathologist, recognized cystic fibrosis. (A pathologist studies diseases.) Anderson earned the degree of doctor of medical science in 1935 from Columbia University College of Physicians and Surgeons. That same year she was the first medical researcher to recognize the disorder known as cystic fibrosis (a disease of the salivary glands or the pancreas). Anderson devoted much of her life to the further study of this disease, as well as the study of congenital defects of the heart.

Source: Sicherman, Barbara, and Carol Hurd Green, eds., *Notable American Women, The Modern Period: A Biographical Dictionary.* Cambridge, Massachusetts: Belknap Press, 1980, pp. 18-20.

1938 ▪ **Katherine Burr Blodgett** (1898-1979), an American chemist, invented nonreflective glass, a glass still used in camera and optical equipment. During World War II (1939-1945) Blodgett also made breakthroughs in airplane wing deicing, and she designed a smoke screen that saved numerous lives in

military campaigns. After the war Blodgett developed an instrument that could be placed in weather balloons to measure humidity in the upper atmosphere. The first female researcher hired by the General Electric Company (GE), Blodgett developed all of her innovations while working for GE. She was awarded the prestigious Francis P. Garvan medal by the American Chemical Society in 1951.

Source: McMurray, Emily J., ed., *Notable Twentieth-Century Scientists.* Detroit: Gale Research, 1995, p. 199.

1938 ▪ Annie Jump Cannon (1863-1941), an American astronomer, was the first woman to hold the post of William Cranch Bond Astronomer at Harvard University. (An astronomer studies stars and other celestial bodies.) Cannon was given the pretigious position for her work in simplifying the existing system of astronomical classification and for her work in cataloguing stars.

Source: Bailey, Brooke, *The Remarkable Lives of 100 Women Healers and Scientists.* Holbrook, Massachusetts: Bob Adams, 1994, pp. 36-37.

1939 ▪ **Hattie Elizabeth Alexander** (1901-1968), an American microbiologist, developed a serum for combating influenza meningitis. (A microbiologist studies microscopic life, or microorganisms.) Alexander earned a medical degree from Johns Hopkins University in 1930. In 1939 she won international recognition for deriving a serum (the watery portion of blood left after blood clotting) to combat influenza meningitis. (This is a form of meningitis, a disease that causes inflammation of the brain and the spinal chord.) Before Alexander's discovery the disease was common and nearly always fatal to infants and young children. In 1964 Alexander became one of the first women to head a national medical association when she was elected president of the American Pediatric Society.

Source: Sicherman, Barbara, and Carol Hurd Green, eds., *Notable American Women: The Modern Period.* Cambridge, Massachusetts: Belknap Press, 1980, pp. 10-11.

1939 ▪ **Pearl Luella Kendrick** (1890-1980), an American microbiologist, and physician Grace Eldening codeveloped a vaccine for pertussis (whooping cough). (A microbiologist studies microscopic life, or microorganisms. A vaccine is a preparation composed of microorganisms that will produce immunity to a disease.) They conducted their experiments while working at the Michigan Department of Health. Kendrick went on to develop the combined immunization DPT (diphtheria, pertussis, and tetanus) vaccine, which virtually eradicated these childhood diseases from the Western world.

Source: Uglow, Jennifer S., *The Continuum Dictionary of Women's Biography.* New York: Continuum, 1989, p. 297.

1939 ▪ **Marguerite Catherine Perey** (1909-1975), a French physicist, discovered francium, the eighty-seventh element in the Periodic Table. (Francium, a rare, highly unstable, radioactive element, is the heaviest chemical of the alkali metal group.) Perey began her career as an assistant to Nobel Prize-winning radiochemist Marie Curie (1867-1934) at the Radium Institute in Paris, France. Perey's work on francium led to her admission to the French Academy of Sciences in 1962. Perey was the first woman to be admitted to the two hundred-year-old Academy (even Curie, winner of two Nobel Prizes, had been unable to break the gender barrier there).

Source: Parry, Melanie, ed., *Larousse Dictionary of Women*. New York: Larousse Kingfisher Chambers, Inc., 1995, p. 520.

1939 ▪ **Harriet Hardy** (1905-1993), an American pathologist, discovered beryllium poisoning. Hardy earned a medical degree from Cornell University in 1932. In 1939 she became the director of health education at Radcliffe College in Cambridge, Massachusetts. In the early 1940s, Hardy conducted research on a strange respiratory disease that developed among the workers in fluorescent lamp factories in nearby Lynn and Salem, Massachusetts. She finally found that dust or vapor from beryllium (a light metal used in the manufacture of fluorescent lamps) could be easily inhaled by factory workers. Hardy became an expert in beryllium poisoning. She also established a registry of berylliosis cases at the Massachusetts General Hospital. This registry later served as a model for the tracking of other occupation-related disorders. In 1954 Hardy was among the first scientists to identify a link between asbestos and cancer.

Chemist Dorothy Crowfoot Hodgkin was the first person to use a computer to analyze a biochemical problem.

Source: *The New York Times.* October 15, 1993.

c. 1940s ▪ **Dorothy Crowfoot Hodgkin** (1910-), an American chemist, was the first person to use a computer to analyze a biochemical problem. During World War II (1939-1945), Hodgkin used computer technology to study the structures of penicillin (an antibiotic) and vitamin B12. Over the course of her career, Hodgkin received numerous awards and honors. In 1964 she became the third woman to receive the Nobel Prize for chemistry. In 1965 she received the Order of Merit, the first woman so honored since nursing pioneer Florence Nightingale (1820-1910). Hodgkin was also the first Wolfson Research Professor of the Royal Society, a post she held from 1960 until

1977. In 1968 she was the first woman to be elected a Fellow of the Australian Academy of Science.

Source: Haber, Louis, *Women Pioneers of Science*. New York: Harcourt Brace Jovanovich, 1979, pp. 105-16.

1940 ▪ Edith Hinkley Quimby (1891-1982), an American biophysicist, was the first woman to receive the Janeway Medal from the American Radium Society. Quimby earned a master's degree in physics from the University of California in 1915. In 1919 she began working with Gioacchino Failla, chief physicist at the newly created New York City Memorial Hospital for Cancer and Allied Diseases, where she became a pioneer in the field of radiology. Quimby helped develop diagnostic and therapeutic applications for X-rays, radium, and radioactive isotopes when the science of radiology was still in its infancy. Her research in measuring the penetration of radiation enabled physicians to determine the exact dose needed with the fewest side effects. Quimby also worked to protect those handling radioactive material from its harmful effects. While a radiology professor at Columbia University, she established a research laboratory to study the medical uses of radioactive isotopes, including their application in cancer diagnosis and treatment.

Source: McMurray, Emily J., ed., *Notable Twentieth-Century Scientists*. Detroit: Gale Research, 1995, pp. 1629-30.

1940 ▪ Eleanor Josephine Macdonald (1906-), an American epidemiologist (a scientist who studies the number of causes, the distribution, and ways to control diseases), established the first cancer registry. After graduating from college with a degree in English and music, MacDonald began her career as a professional cellist. When a physician friend of her father's requested her help writing a research paper, MacDonald was inspired to become an epidemiologist. Taking a job with the Massachusetts Department of Public Health, she began a series of studies on cancer. In 1940 MacDonald developed the first population-based cancer registry (a statistical compilation of the number of cases of cancer within particular geographic regions. Previously, epidemiologists had researched only communicable diseases.) During a career that lasted more than 50 years, she also established a connection between sunlight and malignant melanoma (cancer) of the skin. In addition, she helped increase the awareness of symptoms and treatability of the disease. Macdonald is now considered the first cancer epidemiologist.

Source: McMurray, Emily J., ed., *Notable Twentieth-Century Scientists.* Detroit: Gale Research, 1995, pp. 1293-95.

1942 ▪ Florence Barbara Seibert (1897-1991), an American biochemist, developed a tuberculosis skin test. (A biochemist studies chemical compounds in living organisms. Tuberculosis is a lesion-, or sore-, producing infectious disease most often found in the lungs.) At the age of three, Seibert contracted polio (a viral disease that can cause swelling along the spinal cord and possible paralysis), but with the help of her parents she graduated from Goucher College with a degree in chemistry and zoology in 1918. In 1932, while working at the Henry Phipps Institute in Philadelphia, Pennsylvania, Seibert developed the protein substance used for the tuberculosis skin test. It was adopted as a health standard in 1941 by the United States and a year later by the World Health Organization (WHO). As a graduate student at Yale University (where she earned a Ph.D. in 1923), Seibert invented a distillation (water purification) device that prevented bacterial infection during intravenous injections (injection of medication into the body through a vein). This research later had great practical significance when intravenous blood transfusions became widely used in surgery. (An intravenous drug transfusion involves putting blood into the body through a vein.)

Source: *The New York Times.* August 31, 1991.

Kathleen Yardley Lonsdale was the first female Fellow of the Royal Society.

1945 ▪ Kathleen Yardley Lonsdale (1903-1971), an Irish scientist specializing in physical chemistry (especially the study of crystals), became the first female Fellow of the Royal Society, in London, England. Lonsdale was honored for research

Biochemist Gerty Radnitz
Cori was the first American
woman to win the Nobel
Prize for medicine.

that led to the development of X-ray crystallography. The youngest of ten children and the daughter of an Irish postmaster, Lonsdale was the first scientist to use Fourier analysis to study molecular structures. When the Royal Society agreed to elect woman fellows, Lonsdale was the first one elected.

Source: Magnusson, Magnus, *Larousse Biographical Dictionary*. New York: Larousse Kingfisher Chambers, Inc., 1994, p. 912.

1947 ▪ Gerty Radnitz Cori (1896-1957), a Hungarian-born American biochemist, was the first American woman to win the Nobel Prize for physiology, or medicine. She shared this honor with her husband, Carl Cori (1896-1984), and with Bernardo Houssay of Argentina. The Coris were the third husband- and-wife team to win a Nobel Prize. (The first two were the Curies in 1903 and the Joliet-Curies in 1935.) Gerty and Carl Cori were both on the faculty of the Medical School at Washington University in St. Louis. The Coris were recognized for several discoveries, including the synthesis (mixing) of glycogen (a carbohydrate chemical) in a test tube.

Source: Parry, Melanie, ed., *Larousse Dictionary of Women*. New York: Larousse Kingfisher Chambers, Inc., 1995, p. 161.

c. 1948 ▪ Agnes Robertson Arber (1879-1960) was the first female botanist elected as a Fellow of the Royal Society in England. Arber was honored for her extensive and authoritative work with herbs, water plants, and plant morphology (a branch of biology that deals with the form and structure of plants).

Source: Uglow, Jennifer S., ed., *The Continuum Dictionary of Women's Biography*. New York: Continuum, 1989, p. 25.

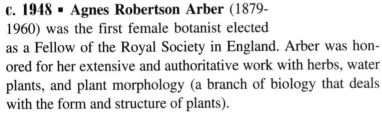

In 1991 Gertrude B. Elion was the first woman inducted into the National Inventors Hall of Fame in Akron, Ohio.

1950 ▪ Gertrude B. Elion (1918-), an American biochemist, was the first person to develop a drug that attacked viruses. (A biochemist studies chemical compounds in living organisms.) Elion made this scientific advance while working at the Burroughs Wellcome Company laboratory in Tuckahoe, New York. Her discovery was important for the treatment of cancer and AIDS (Acquired Immune Deficiency Syndrome). In 1988 Elion and her colleague, George Hitchings (1905-), shared the Nobel Prize for physiology, or medicine. In 1991 Elion was the first woman inducted into the National Inventors Hall of Fame in

Friend's Discovery

Charlotte Friend (1921-1987), a U.S. microbiologist who devoted her career to cancer research, was the first person to discover that a virus can cause leukemia (a disease of the blood) in mammals. Friend did most of her research at the Sloan-Kettering Institute for Cancer Research and at the Experimental Cell Biology Center at Mt. Sinai School of Medicine in New York City.

Akron, Ohio. She was honored for her many achievements in the field of drug research.

Source: McGrayne, Sharon Bertsch, *Nobel Prize Women in Science: Their Lives, Struggles and Momentous Discoveries.* New York: Birch Lane Press, 1993, pp. 280-83.

1951 ▪ **Rosalind Franklin** (1920-1958), an English microchemist, was the first person to discover the helical structure of DNA (the basic unit of genetic identity). Franklin was part of a four-member team that eventually shared credit for the discovery of the "double helix" form. Following her untimely death, Maurice Wilkins (1916-), James Watson (1928-), and Francis Crick (1916-) received a Nobel Prize for the team's discovery, in 1962. The work of this team of scientists is considered the beginning of the discipline of molecular biology.

Source: Judson, Horace Freeland, *The Eighth Day of Creation: Makers of the Revolution in Biology.* New York: Simon and Schuster, 1980.

1952 ▪ **Mildred Trotter** (1899-1991), an American anatomist, developed a bone-height formula. In 1948 Trotter was the volunteer director of the Central Identification Laboratory in Oahu, Hawaii, where she identified skeletal remains of World War II (1939-1945) dead. She conducted allometric (growth pattern) studies using the long limb bones of identified dead, one of the first times that war casualties were used for scientific research. From these studies Trotter then devised a formula for estimating the stature of a person based upon the relative length of the long bones. In 1956 she became the first female recipient of the Wenner-Gren Foundation's Viking Fund Medal.

Source: Wood, W. Raymond, and Lori Ann Stanley, "Recovery and Identification of World War II Dead: American Graves Registration Activities in Europe," *Journal of Forensic Sciences.* Volume 34, 1989, pp. 1365-73.

1958 ▪ **Chien Shiung Wu** (1912-), a Chinese-born American nuclear physicist, was the first woman to receive an honorary doctorate in science from Princeton University, in 1958.

In 1941 Wu became the first woman to teach at Princeton. She was also the first woman to win the Comstock Prize from the National Academy of Sciences in the late 1950s, the first woman to receive the Wolf Prize from Israel, and the first female president of the American Physical Society. In 1972 Wu became the first person to hold the Pupin Professorship in Physics at Columbia University.

Source: Vare, Ethlie, and Greg Ptacek, *Mothers of Invention: From the Bra to the Bomb, Forgotten Women and Their Unforgettable Ideas.* New York: William Morrow, 1988, pp. 153-57.

Chien Shiung Wu was the first woman to win the Comstock Prize from the National Academy of Sciences.

1958 ▪ Désirée Le Beau (1907-1993), an Austro-Hungarian chemist, pioneered rubber recycling. Le Beau earned a Ph.D. in chemistry from the University of Graz in Austria in 1931. Five years later she moved to the U.S. and worked as a research chemist. In 1945 she was appointed director of research at Midwest Rubber Reclaiming Company in Illinois, where she developed methods of reclaiming (recycling) natural and synthetic rubbers—primarily from old tires—to be used in producing new products. Recycling was especially important because rubber supplies had been depleted during World War II (1939-1945). Among Le Beau's innovations was a railroad tie pad made from recycled rubber, for which she obtained a patent in 1958. Le Beau also held patents for several recycling processes. She was the first woman to chair the American Chemical Society's Division of Colloid Chemistry.

Source: McMurray, Emily J., ed., *Notable Twentieth-Century Scientists.* Detroit: Gale Research, 1995, pp. 1198-99.

1963 ▪ Maria Goeppert-Mayer (1906-1972) was the first American woman to win the Nobel Prize for physics. Sharing the honor with two men (Eugene Paul Wigner and Hans Jensen), Goeppert-Mayer was awarded the prize on December 10, 1963, for her work on the theory of the stability of atomic nuclei.

Source: Haber, Louis, *Women Pioneers of Science.* New York: Harcourt Brace Jovanovich, 1979, pp. 83-96.

c. 1965 ▪ **Berta Scharrer** (1906-1995), a German-born American biologist, established the concept of neurosecretion. (Neurosecretion is the study of the interaction of the nervous system and endocrine system. The endocrine system consists of glands that secrete hormones.) Scharrer earned a Ph.D. from the University of Munich in 1930; four years later she married Ernst Albert Scharrer, a biologist. The couple formed an intellectual and domestic partnership that lasted until Ernst Scharrer's death in 1965. During her career, Scharrer conducted experiments on the South American cockroach and other invertebrates (animals without spines). She was able to prove that nerve cells not only conduct electricity, but that they also control the release of hormones. Scharrer was honored with a National Medal of Science in 1983.

Source: Parry, Melanie, ed., *Larousse Dictionary of Women.* New York: Larousse Kingfisher Chambers, Inc., 1995, p. 585.

1967 ▪ **Jocelyn Susan Bell Burnell** (1943-), an Irish astronomer, discovered pulsars. Bell Burnell made the discovery while working on her Ph.D. under Anthony Hewish at Cambridge University in England. She had chosen to do her doctoral work on recently discovered quasars (star formations the size of galaxies that are so distant from the Earth that they appear to be single stars). While listening to signals on a radio telescope, Bell Burnell noticed some curious variations. Soon Bell Burnell, Hewish, and other researchers realized that the intermittent signals were coming from a neutron star. Hewish named that the source "pulsating star," and that the term was soon contracted to pulsar, because that the star pulsated (pulsed or "vibrated") at regular intervals. Hewish was awarded that the Nobel Prize in 1974 for this discovery, though Bell Burnell was not included in that citation. She received that the Herschel Medal of Science in 1989.

Source: Parry, Melanie, ed., *Larousse Dictionary of Women.* New York: Larousse Kingfisher Chambers, Inc., 1995, p. 67.

Late 1960s ▪ Rita Rossi Colwell (1934-), an American marine biologist (a person who studies organisms in oceans and seas), codiscovered the bacterium that causes cholera. (A bacterium is a disease-causing organism. Cholera is a disease affecting the stomach and intestinal tract.) After earning a Ph.D. in marine biology from the University of Washington, Seattle, in 1961, Colwell headed a research team at Georgetown University. In the late 1960s the team found that the cholera bacterium grows naturally in estuaries. (An estuary is an arm of the sea at the lower end of a river.) This important breakthrough led to better understanding and treatment of cholera. Colwell went on to become a founder and president of the University of Maryland Biotechnology Institute.

Source: Andrews, Joan Kostick, "Lady with a Mission," *Natural Science.* May, 1991, pp. 304-10.

c. 1972 ▪ Vera Cooper Rubin (1928-), an American astronomer, codiscovered the possible existence of dark matter in the universe. (An astronomer studies stars and other celestial bodies. "Dark matter" refers to substances that are not visible or detectable as they are, but are presumed to exist because the visible matter is not sufficient to explain certain gravitational effects.) Rubin earned a doctorate in astronomy from Georgetown University in 1954. Nine years later she joined the Department of Terrestrial Magnetism (DTM) at Carnegie Institute. Rubin and DTM physicist W. Kent Ford used a spectrograph (an instrument that breaks down light, radiation, or sound waves into their component parts and photographs the resulting spectrum, or array) to study the rate of rotation within galaxies. During their studies, the researchers discovered the existence of dark matter, which has significantly advanced man's knowledge of the universe.

Source: McMurray, Emily J., ed., *Notable Twentieth-Century Scientists.* Detroit: Gale Research, 1995, p. 1726.

1972 ▪ Margaret Eleanor Burbidge (1920-), a British astronomer, was the first female director of the Royal Greenwich Observatory in Greenwich, England. During her tenure from 1972-1973, Burbidge was denied the traditional title of

"Astronomer Royal" because of her gender. Burbidge went on to become the first female president of the American Astronomical Society (1976-1978) and the American Association for the Advancement of Science (1981).

Source: Uglow, Jennifer S., ed., *The Continuum Dictionary of Women's Biography.* New York: Continuum, 1989, pp. 95-96.

1973 ▪ **Candace Dorinda Bebe Pert** (1946-), an American neuroscientist, codiscovered opiate receptors in the brain. (A neuroscientist studies the nervous system of an organism.) As a graduate student at Johns Hopkins University in 1973, Pert codiscovered the brain's opiate receptors (areas that react to painkilling substances such as morphine). Her work led to the discovery of endorphins (naturally occurring substances manufactured in the brain that relieve pain and produce sensations of pleasure). In 1986 Pert led the National Institutes of Mental Health (NIMH) team that discovered peptide T. (Peptides are substances that are synthesized from amino acids and have been linked to the manifestation of emotions.) For her discoveries, Pert won the Arthur S. Fleming Award in 1979.

Source: Weintraub, Pamela, ed., *The Omni Interviews.* New York: Omni Press, pp. 118-31.

1975 ▪ **Rachel Fuller Brown** (1898-1980) was the first woman to receive the Pioneer Chemist Award from the American Institute of Chemists. Brown was honored for her discovery of a pneumonia vaccine in the 1920s and for her work with Elizabeth Hazer to isolate the first antifungal antibiotic in 1950.

Source: Haber, Louis, *Women Pioneers of Science.* New York: Harcourt Brace Jovanovich, 1979, pp. 63-72.

1976 ▪ **Rosalyn S. Yalow** (1921-), a physicist working in medicine, was the first woman to receive the Albert Lasker Basic Medical Research Award. Yalow was honored for her pioneering work in the field of radioimmunoassay, a new method for the precise measurement of substances in the blood. In 1977 she became the first American-born woman to receive a Nobel Prize in science.

Source: Noble, Iris, *Contemporary Women Scientists of America.* New York: Julian Messner, 1979, pp. 128-40.

1976 ▪ **Julia Bowman Robinson** (1920-1985), an American mathematician, was the first female mathematician elected to the National Academy of Sciences. Robinson was honored for her work solving logic problems by using number theories. In 1948 she earned a doctorate in mathematics from the University of California. She then continued her work on the last of the "ten problems for the twentieth century" posed by the German mathematician David Hilbert (1862-1943) in 1900. From 1948 to 1968 Robinson developed the framework on which the solution was constructed in 1970.

Source: Read, Phyllis J., and Bernard L. Witlieb, *The Book of Women's Firsts.* New York: Random House, 1992, p. 375.

1976 ▪ **Cecilia Payne-Gaposchkin** (1900-1979), an English-born American astronomer, was the first woman to receive the Henry Norris Russell Prize from the American Astronomical Society. Payne-Gaposchkin was honored for her work as a pioneer in the field of astronomy. After earning a Ph.D. in astronomy from Harvard University in 1925, Payne-Gaposchkin was the first researcher to conclude that hydrogen and helium, the two lightest elements, were also the two most common elements in the universe. In 1925 she revealed that hydrogen, the simplest of the known elements, was the most abundant substance in the universe. Payne-Gaposchkin's findings have since become the basis for analysis of the cosmos, yet she has never been officially credited with the discoveries (which she made as a doctoral candidate). In 1977 the minor planet "1974-CA" was named in honor of Payne-Gaposchkin.

Source: Kass-Simon, G., and Patricia Farnes, *Women of Science: Righting the Record.* Bloomington, Indiana: Indiana University Press, 1990.

1977 ▪ **Xide Xie** (1921-), a Chinese physicist, founded the Modern Physics Institute in Shanghai, China. With a doctorate in her field from the Massachusetts Institute of Technology (MIT), Xie established her career at Fudan University and at the Institute of Technical Physics, both in Shanghai.

Source: Uglow, Jennifer S., ed., *The Continuum Dictionary of Women's Biography.* New York: Continuum, 1989, p. 594.

Bernstein Elected President

Dorothy Lewis Bernstein (1914-), an American mathematician, was the first female president of the Mathematical Association of America. This national organization was concerned with the teaching of college mathematics. After joining the faculty at Goucher College in Baltimore, Maryland, in 1959, Bernstein was a pioneer in incorporating applied mathematics and computer science into the undergraduate mathematics curriculum.

c. 1978 ▪ **Helen Thom Edwards** (1936-), an American physicist, designed the Tevatron. Edwards earned a Ph.D. in physics from Cornell University in 1966. Four years later she became associate head of the Booster Group at Fermi National Accelerator Laboratory, also known as "Fermilab." In 1978 Edwards was put in charge of designing and building a superconducting proton accelerator called the Tevatron. (Protons are positively charged elementary particles. An accelerator is a device used to give high velocity to protons.) The first successful superconducting proton accelerator, Tevatron is still the most powerful accelerator in operation.

Source: Lederman, Leon, and Dick Teresi, *The God Particle.* New York: Houghton Mifflin, 1993.

1986 ▪ **Margaret Joan Geller** (1947-), an American astronomer (a person who studies stars and other celestial bodies), codiscovered the "Great Wall" of galaxies. Geller received a Ph.D in astronomy from Princeton University in 1975. Beginning in 1980 she collaborated with astronomer John P. Huchra on a large-scale survey of galaxies (large groups of stars). Scientists have long predicted that galaxies are uniformly distributed in space. Geller and Huchra proposed that a three-dimensional mapping of galaxies would confirm this uniformity. In 1986 the duo published their first results.

Instead of the expected distribution, however, the researchers' "slice" of the cosmos showed sheets of galaxies appearing to line the walls of bubble-like empty spaces. Geller and Huchra's so-called "Great Wall" is a system of thousands of galaxies arranged across the universe, containing about five times the average density of galaxies. Between 1986 and 1989, Geller and Huchra published four maps, and their survey will eventually plot about 15,000 galaxies.

Source: Bartusiak, "Mapping the Universe," *Discover.* August 1, 1990, pp. 60-63.

c. 1990 ▪ **Rita Levi-Montalcini** (1909-), an Italian-born American neurobiologist, was the first woman admitted to the Pontifical Academy of Sciences in Rome, Italy. (A neurobiologist studies the nervous system.) Levi-Montalcini was recognized for her work in neuroembryology, for which she also received the Nobel Prize in physiology, or medicine, in 1986. In the 1950s she discovered nerve growth factor (NGF), a protein in the nervous system. Collaborating with biochemist Stanley Cohen at Washington University, Levi-Montalcini eventually isolated NGF. The duo's work later proved useful in the study of several disorders, including Alzheimer's disease, cancer, and birth defects.

Source: McGrayne, Sharon Bertsch, *Nobel Prize Women in Science: Their Lives, Struggles and Momentous Discoveries.* New York: Birch Lane Press, 1993, pp. 201-24.

1991 ▪ **Susan Epstein Leeman** (1930-), an American physiologist, was the first woman elected to the Physiology and Pharmacology Section of the National Academy of Sciences. Leeman was honored for her work as a founder of the field of neuroendocrinology. (A neuroendocrinologist studies the interaction between the nervous system and the endocrine, or hormone-producing, system). After receiving a Ph.D. in physiology from Harvard University Medical School in 1958, Leeman conducted pioneering work with peptides. (A peptide is a substance derived from two or more amino acids.) Early in her career she isolated substance P, which had been discovered in the 1930s, but had never been isolated. (Distributed throughout the central and peripheral nervous systems as well as the spinal cord, substance P has many functions in the human body.) During her work with substance P, Leeman discovered another peptide, neuro-tensin, which is found in both the central nervous system and the gastrointestinal tract.

Source: McMurray, Emily J., ed., *Notable Twentieth-Century Scientists.* Detroit: Gale Research, 1995, pp. 1212-13.

1994 ▪ **Mary-Claire King,** an American genetic researcher, was the first person to prove breast cancer is genetic. The sister and sister-in-law of breast cancer patients, King treated her research as a personal crusade. In 1975 she first theorized that breast cancer genes existed. More recently, King has been researching the protein encoded by the breast cancer gene. Her eventual intention is to discover a drug that will alter the effect of the gene.

Source: Bell, Lisa, "Mary-Claire King: The First to Prove Breast Cancer is Genetic," *Working Woman.* November-December, 1996, p. 50.

Technical Science

1898 ▪ Hertha Marks Ayrton (1854-1923), an English physicist, became the first woman elected to the Institution of Electrical Engineers in England. In 1906 she won the Hughes Medal, becoming the first woman to be awarded a medal by the Royal Society (Ayrton was honored for her work on the motion of waves and formation of sand ripples). She was also the inventor of a sphygmograph, an instrument used to measure the pulse. During World War I (1914-1918), Ayrton invented the "Ayrton Fan" for clearing poisonous gases. Although she completed her studies at Cambridge University in 1881, Ayrton was not awarded a degree because women were not permitted to receive degrees at the time.

Source: Ogilvie, Marilyn Bailey, *Women in Science: Antiquity through the Nineteenth Century.* Cambridge, Massachusetts: M.I.T. Press, 1986, pp. 32-34.

1945 ▪ Grace Brewster Murray Hopper (1906-1992), an American mathematician, was the first person to develop operating programs for the first digital computer. She originated the concept of automatic programming from which the first English-language compiler system was incorporated into the widely used Common Business Oriented Language (COBOL). She did this work for the U.S. Navy after enlisting in the WAVES (Women Accepted for Voluntary Emergency Service) during World War II (1939-1945). Holding a Ph.D. in mathematics from Yale University (1934), Hopper went on to a distinguished career in computer science. Although she retired from the Navy in 1966, she remained active in her field. In 1973 she became the first person in the Naval Reserve to be promoted (to the rank of captain in her case) while on the retired list.

Source: Read, Phyllis J., and Bernard L. Witlieb, *The Book of Women's Firsts.* New York: Random House, 1992, pp. 214-15.

1950 ▪ **Beatrice Hicks** (1919-1979), an American engineer, cofounded the Society of Women Engineers (SWE) and was elected its first president. She also served as director of the First International Conference of Women Engineers and Scientists, organized by the SWE and held in New York in 1964. A graduate of the Newark College of Engineering (1939), Hicks was president of Newark Controls Company, which was founded by her father in New Jersey. Hicks invented the gas density switch, an integral part of systems using artificial atmospheres. In 1963 Hicks became the first woman to be awarded an honorary doctorate of engineering by Rensselaer Polytechnic Institute.

Source: McMurray, Emily J., ed., *Notable Twentieth-Century Scientists.* Detroit: Gale Research, 1995, p. 924.

1952 ▪ **Maria Telkes** (1900-), a Hungarian-born American physical chemist, received the first Society of Women Engineers Achievement Award. She was recognized for her contributions to solar energy research. Telkes received a Ph.D. in chemistry from Budapest University in 1924 and joined the Massachusetts Institute of Technology (M.I.T.) Solar Energy Conversion Project in 1939. During her career Telkes designed solar ovens, solar stills, and solar electric generators. She was also responsible for developing the heating system installed in the first solar-heated home, located in Dover, Massachusetts.

Source: O'Neill, Lois Decker, ed., *The Woman's Book of World Records and Achievements.* New York: Doubleday, 1979, p. 189.

c. 1953 ▪ **Jessie Gambrioni Cambra** (1919-), an American engineer, developed and supervised the first successful highway reconstruction project in California. Cambra was also responsible for the design of the first computerized integrated traffic signal system in a major highway intersection. She did this work during her tenure as a chief engineer in Alameda County, California, an affiliation that lasted until her retirement in 1979. In 1942 Cambra was the first woman to graduate with a degree in civil engineering. (A civil engineer designs public works such as highways and harbors.)

Source: *The Engineer in America: A Historical Analogy from Technology to Culture.* Chicago: University of Chicago Press, 1991.

1954 ▪ **Mary G. Ross** (1908-), a Native-American aerospace engineer, was the only woman working in the first Lockheed Missiles Systems Division. A 1928 graduate of Northeastern State Teacher's College in 1928, Ross took a position at Lockheed Aircraft Corporation in Burbank, California, in 1942. She then enrolled in aeronautical and mechanical engineering courses at the University of California. When Lockheed formed the Missiles Systems Division in 1954, Ross was selected to be one of the first forty employees and the only woman on the team. She conducted research on ballistic missiles and other defense systems, as well as the effects of ocean waves on submarine-launched vehicles. Beginning in 1958 Ross worked on satellite orbits and the Agena series of rockets that played a prominent role in the Apollo moon program. She was eventually elected a fellow and life member of the Society of Women Engineers. In 1992 she was inducted into the Silicon Valley Engineering Hall of Fame.

Source: McMurray, Emily J., ed., *Notable Twentieth-Century Scientists.* Detroit: Gale Research, 1995, pp. 1710-11.

c. 1970s ▪ **Ada Irene Pressman** (1927-), an American engineer, developed a secondary cooling system for nuclear power plants. (A nuclear power plant makes electricity from atomic fission.) During the 1970s, as a project engineer at Bechtel Corporation in Los Angles, California, Pressman designed the nuclear plant cooling system. The device operates from a diesel generator in the event of a primary power source loss. It protects people working at a plant site against the danger of radiation and protects plant machinery from physical damage if malfunctions occur. Pressman earned an undergraduate engineering degree from the Ohio State University in 1950 and a master's degree in business administration at Golden Gate University in 1974. For her achievements Pressman received the Society of Women Engineers Annual Achievement Award in 1976.

Source: McMurray, Emily J., ed., *Notable Twentieth-Century Scientists.* Detroit: Gale Research, 1995, pp. 1616-17.

1971 ▪ **Irmgard Flügge-Lotz** (1903-1974), a German-born American engineer, was the first woman chosen by the American Institute of Aeronautics and Astronautics (AIAA) to deliver the prestigious annual von Karman Lecture; the AIAA also elected her as its first woman fellow. Flügge-Lotz held a doctorate in engineering from the Technical University of Hanover, Germany. Early in her career, while working at the Aerodynamische Veruchsanstalt research institute in Germany during World War II (1939-1945), she developed the "Lotz-method." (A technique for calculating the lift distribution on aircraft wings, the procedure is still in use today.) After the war Flügge-Lotz joined the staff at Stanford University in Palo Alto, California. In 1960 she became the first woman professor of aeronautics and astronautics, as well as engineering mechanics, at Stanford.

Source: McMurray, Emily J., ed., *Notable Twentieth-Century Scientists.* Detroit: Gale Research, 1995, pp. 662-63.

c. 1980s ▪ **Adele Goldberg** (1945-), an American computer scientist, codeveloped Smalltalk. While working at the Xerox Corporation in the 1970s, Goldberg began a collaboration with computer engineer Alan Kay and other computer scientists. During the 1980s the team invented a set of programming tools and a user interface (a means of communication between the computer user and computer programs). This technique was the first to use pictures that allowed programmers to interact with overlapping windows on the computer screen. (Previously, computer users were required to type in keyboard commands.) In 1990 Goldberg, who held a doctorate in information sciences from the University of Chicago (1973), received the *PC Magazine* Lifetime Achievement Award.

Source: Garber, Joseph R., "Working Faster," *Forbes.* April 12, 1993, p. 10.

1980 ▪ **Lynn Ann Conway** (1938-), an American computer engineer, invented a new method for making computer chips. While working at the Xerox Corporation she published a description of the technique in *Introduction to VLSI Systems* in 1980. As a result, computer program designers could very rapidly obtain models with which to test their hardware (electronic devices) and software (computer program) inventions. Conway began her career after receiving a master's degree in electrical engineering from Columbia University in 1963. During the 1970s she helped create a method that allowed computer engineers without specialized expertise to design integrated computer circuit chips. (A computer chip is a tiny piece of silicon, a non-metal material, that conducts electricity. The chip contains integrated circuits, or a large number of miniaturized electronic components.) Conway received the Major Educational Innovation Award from the Institute of Electrical and Electronics Engineers.

Source: McMurray, Emily J., ed., *Notable Twentieth-Century Scientists.* Detroit: Gale Research, 1995, pp. 392-93.

c. 1992 ▪ **Elsa Reichmanis** (1953-), an Australian-born chemist, developed Camp-6. Camp-6 was a "resist" material used in the 1990s to make the next generation of integrated computer circuits smaller and more powerful than ever before. (A resist material is composed of organic polymers, a mixture of chemical compounds that produces repeated structural units. An integrated circuit is a large number of related electronic components.) Holding a Ph.D. in organic chemistry from Syracuse University (1975), Reichmanis obtained eleven patents for the design and development of the organic polymers used in microlithography. (Microlithography is the principal process by which circuits, or electrical pathways, are imprinted upon the tiny silicon chips that drive computers.) She did all of her work at the AT&T Bell Laboratories in New Jersey. In 1993 Reichmanis received the Society of Woman Engineers Annual Achievement Award for her contributions in the field of integrated circuitry.

Source: McMurray, Emily J., ed., *Notable Twentieth-Century Scientists.* Detroit: Gale Research, 1995, pp. 1660-61.

Space Exploration

1960 ▪ **Geraldyn (Jerrie) Cobb** (1931-), an African-American aviator, was the first woman to qualify as a U.S. astronaut. She passed the 75 required exams in February of 1960, but was denied the opportunity to go into space because she was a woman. In 1963 Cobb urged President Lyndon B. Johnson (served in office 1963-1969) to appoint her as the first female astronaut. Later that year, Cobb was one of three women recommended for astronaut service. The National Aeronautics and Space Administration (NASA) was not yet ready to accept women in this capacity, however, and rejected all three female candidates.

Source: Read, Phyllis J., and Bernard L. Witlieb, *The Book of Women's Firsts*. New York: Random House, 1992, pp. 94-95.

c. 1962 ▪ **Alla Genrikhovna Massevitch** (1918-), a Russian astronomer, was the first Russian woman to be put in charge of tracking space vehicles. A professor of astrophysics (a specialized branch of astronomy) at Moscow University beginning in 1948, Massevitch began specializing in tracking space vehicles through the use of visual, photographic, and laser techniques during the early 1960s.

Source: Uglow, Jennifer S., ed., *The Continuum Dictionary of Women's Biography*. New York: Continuum, 1989, p. 365.

1963 ▪ **Valentina Tereshkova** (1937-), a Russian cosmonaut, was the first woman in space, and only the tenth human being to orbit the earth. Before joining the cosmonaut program in 1962, Tereshkova was an amateur parachutist. She was the solo pilot of the spaceship, *Vostok VI,* which was launched on June 16, 1963. Tereshkova orbited the earth 48 times, traveling over 1.2 million miles before returning to earth three days later. Tereshkova went on to a distinguished career as a representative of her country on diplomatic missions.

Source: Magnusson, Magnus, *Larousse Biographical Dictionary*. Edinburgh: Larousse Kingfisher Chambers, Inc., 1994, p. 1442.

c. 1970s ▪ **Nancy Grace Roman** (1925-), an American astronomer, invented satellite observatories. Roman received a

doctorate in astronomy in 1949 from the University of Chicago. (An astronomer studies stars and other celestial bodies.) In 1959 Roman became head of the astronomy program at the National Aeronautics and Space Administration (NASA) in Washington, D.C. She then developed a plan to observe objects in space by using rockets and satellite observatories. Roman improved her orbiting observatories throughout the

1970s and 1980s. As part of her research, she measured X-ray and ultraviolet readings from the successful OAO-3 or *Copernicus* satellite, which was launched in 1972. Roman's programs also led to the successful *Viking* space probes designed to collect data from Mars in 1976.

Source: O'Neill, Lois Decker, ed., *The Women's Book of World Records and Achievements.* New York: Doubleday, 1979, pp. 88, 153.

c. 1970s ▪ **Yvonne Claeys Brill** (1924-), a Canadian- born American aerospace engineer, designed a single-propellant rocket system. (A propellant provides thrust or movement. Propellants are found in many household products, such aerosol spray cleaners.) Brill earned a master's degree in chemistry in 1951 from the University of Southern California. During her career, Brill developed new rocket propulsion systems for communications satellites. A single propellant rocket system she developed in the 1970s, and for which she holds the patent, is still in use today. Brill served with the National Aeronautics and Space Administration (NASA) space shuttle program office from 1981 to 1983, and she played a role in developing the propulsion system design for the International Maritime Satellite Organization (INMARSAT). She was awarded the Resnick Challenger Medal in 1993.

Source: Parsons, Susan V., "1993 Resnick Challenger Medal Recipient: Yvonne C. Brill," *SWE.* September-October, 1993, pp. 18-20.

1982 ▪ **Svetlanta Saviskaya,** a Russian cosmonaut, was the first woman to walk in space. She went up in a *Soyuz* T-5 capsule and walked in space while docking with the *Salyut* 7 space station.

Source: Levin, Beatrice, *Women and Medicine: Pioneers Meeting the Challenge!* Lincoln, Nebraska: Media Publishing, 1988, p. 31.

1983 ▪ **Sally Ride** (1951-), an American physicist, was the first American woman to travel in space. In 1978, the same

Seddon Became Astronaut

In 1979 Margaret Rhea Seddon (1947-), an American physician, was the first U.S. woman to achieve the rank of astronaut. She completed her training and evaluation period in August of 1979. Seddon flew her first space mission aboard the shuttle *Discovery* on April 12, 1985.

year she earned a Ph.D. in physics from Stanford University, she was selected for the National Aeronautics and Space Administration (NASA) astronaut program. In June 1983 Ride took a six-day flight aboard the *Challenger* orbiter satellite (a space vehicle that circles the Earth). She also designed the Space Shuttle robot arm (a device that retrieves objects in space). Ride went on to a distinguished career in physics and continues to serve as a spokesperson for space exploration.

Source: Read, Phyllis J., and Bernard L. Witlieb, *The Book of Women's Firsts.* New York: Random House, 1992, pp. 370-71.

1984 ▪ **Kathryn D. Sullivan** (1951-), an American geologist, became the first American woman to participate in extra-vehicular activity in space (that is, going outside the space vehicle in a space suit). Sullivan was one of the first women selected for the National Aeronautics and Space Administration (NASA) space shuttle program. Sullivan completed a doctorate in geology at Dalhousie University in Nova Scotia shortly before joining NASA. During her first mission in October of 1984, she demonstrated the possibility of in-flight satellite refueling. Sullivan flew a second mission on April 24, 1990, during which the Hubble Space Telescope was launched into space.

Source: Read, Phyllis J., and Bernard L. Witlieb, *The Book of Women's Firsts.* New York: Random House, 1992, p. 429.

1992 ▪ **Mae Carol Jemison** (1956-), an American physician and astronaut, was the first African-American space traveler. Jemison obtained a medical degree from Cornell University Medical College in 1981. She was accepted into the National Aeronautics and Space Administration (NASA) astronaut program in 1987. On September 12, 1992, Jemison flew into space with six other astronauts aboard the space shuttle *Endeavor* on mission STS-47. During her eight days in space, she conducted experiments on weightlessness (the lack of gravity) and motion sickness on the crew and herself. In recognition of her accomplishments, Jemison received the *Ebony* Black Achievement Award in 1992.

Source: McMurray, Emily J., ed., *Notable Twentieth-Century Scientists.* Detroit: Gale Research, 1995, pp. 1016- 17.

1992 ▪ **Patricia Suzanne Cowings** (1948-), an African- American research psycho-physiologist (a person who studies how the mind affects biological functions in the body), designed a program to reduce motion-sickness in astronauts. She earned both a master's degree and a doctorate in psychology from the University of California at Davis in 1973. Four years later Cowings joined the National Aeronautics and Space Administration (NASA) as a research psychologist at the Ames Psychophysiological Research Laboratory in California. Cowings began research on what was called the "zero-gravity sickness syndrome." Once NASA had decided to fly a space shuttle and keep its astronaut crews in space for increasingly longer periods, this syndrome—similar to the more common motion sickness—became a real concern. Cowings was asked to devise a program that might help astronauts minimize these symptoms without drugs. Using biofeedback techniques, she conducted experiments with a group of volunteers that resulted in the improvement of their ability to withstand motion sickness. Cowings's work was finally put to use in 1992 during an eight-day flight of the space shuttle *Endeavor*. Members of the crew wore a harness apparatus that successfully monitored their ability to suppress the onset of motion sickness.

Source: *Aviation Week and Space Technology.* September 21, 1992, pp. 24-25.

The *Sojourner* Mars Rover

The *Sojourner* Mars rover was the first U.S. spacecraft to send back live photos for public viewing on the Internet. The rover was named for Sojourner Truth (1797-1883), the African-American woman who fought for women's suffrage (the right to vote) and the abolition (elimination) of slavery. The National Aeronautics and Space Administration (NASA) launched *Sojourner* on the Mars Pathfinder on December 2, 1996. The rover landed on Mars and began its explorations on July 4, 1997.

1993 ▪ **Ellen Ochoa** (1958-), an American engineer, was the first Hispanic female astronaut. After receiving a doctorate in electrical engineering from Stanford University in 1985, she joined Sandia National Laboratories in Livermore, California. Ochoa became a specialist in optics and optical recognition in robotics. In the late 1980s she began working with the National Aeronautics and Space Administration (NASA) as an optical specialist. After leading a project team, Ochoa was selected for the NASA space flight program. Ochoa made her first flight on the space shuttle *Discovery* in April of 1993.

Source: McMurray, Emily J., ed., *Notable Twentieth-Century Scientists.* Detroit: Gale Research, 1995, pp. 1496- 98.

1996 ▪ **Shannon Lucid** (1943-), an American physician, spent the longest time of any person—male or female—in space. Lucid obtained a medical degree from the University of Oklahoma in 1973. In 1978 she became one of the first women selected for the U.S. National Aeronautics and Space Administration (NASA) space shuttle program. Lucid took her first space flight in 1985, then in 1989 she traveled aboard the orbiter *Atlantis,* which deployed the spacecraft *Galileo* on its exploration voyage to the planet Jupiter.

Lucid flew on *Atlantis* again in 1991, making 142 orbits of the earth and logging 21 days in space. Her greatest achievement thus far, however, took place in 1996, when she traveled aboard the Russian space shuttle *Mir.* As a result of her 188-day voyage, Lucid became the American astronaut who spent the longest time in space. Lucid was awarded the Congressional Space Medal of Honor by President Bill Clinton (began term in office in 1993).

Source: Read, Phyllis J., and Bernard L. Witlieb, *The Book of Women's Firsts.* New York: Random House, 1992, p. 429.

Sports

Individual Sports
Team Sports
Travel and Adventure

Individual Sports

1496 ▪ Juliana Berners/Barnes (sometimes listed as Bernes or Berners; b. 1388?), the prioress (head nun) at the abbey of St. Albans in England, was the first female fly fisher on record. The first women's fly fishing club, founded in the United States in 1932, named Berners its "patron saint." The original organization included approximately 90 members, most of whom had been fishing in Catskill streams (in upstate New York) at the turn of the twentieth century. Berners was also the author of *The Book of St. Albans,* a collection of essays on field sports first published in 1496, which included her "Treatyse of Fysshynge Wyth an Angle."

Source: *The New York Times.* August 18, 1994.

1542 ▪ Mary, Queen of Scots (1542-1587) was the first recognized female golfer. Mary openly advocated the game, which originated in Scotland, during her reign (1542-1587).

Constance Applebee, a physical education instructor, introduced field hockey in the United States. (See "Team Sports" entry dated 1901.)

A Female Boxing Match

Nell Saunders defeated Rose Harland in the first women's boxing match in the United States on March 16, 1876.

Source: Sanders, Dennis, *The First of Everything.* New York: Delacorte Press, 1981, p. 218.

1804 ▪ **Alicia Meynell,** an American horseback rider, was the first female jockey. Meynell rode against Captain William Flint in a four-mile race in York, England, on August 25, 1804.

Source: Woolum, Janet, *Outstanding Women Athletes: Who They Are and How They Influenced Sports in America.* Phoenix, Arizona: Oryx Press, 1992, p. 24.

1887 ▪ **Lottie Dod** (1871-1960), known at the age of 12 as "the little wonder," was the first female tennis prodigy (young sensation). In 1887, two months short of her sixteenth birthday, Dod became the first teenager ever to win the women's singles event at the Wimbledon Lawn Tennis Championships in England.

Source: Uglow, Jennifer S., ed., *The Continuum Dictionary of Women's Biography.* New York: Continuum, 1989, p. 171.

1893 ▪ **Margaret Scott** (1875-?) was the first woman to become British Ladies' Golf Champion. She won this title in 1893, the year of the formation of the Ladies' Golf Union (which sponsored golf competition). Scott held the title three times, after which she retired from competitive golf.

Source: Uglow, Jennifer S., ed., *The Continuum Dictionary of Women's Biography.* New York: Continuum, 1989, pp. 488-89.

1902 ▪ **Mrs. Adolph Ladenburg** of Saratoga, New York, introduced an innovative horse show riding outfit when she wore a split skirt rather than the traditional ankle-length dress. Ladenburg also rode her horse astride rather than sidesaddle (one of the first women to do so in public).

Source: Woolum, Janet, *Outstanding Women Athletes: Who They Are and How They Influenced Sports in America.* Phoenix, Arizona: Oryx Press, 1992, p. 25.

1905 ▪ **May Sutton Bundy** (1887-1975), a British tennis player, was the first woman to win the women's singles title at the Wimbledon Lawn Tennis Championships when she defeated Doris K. Douglas of Great Britain. Sutton won the title again in 1907. A competitor until 1928, Sutton was inducted into the International Tennis Hall of Fame in 1956.

Source: Read, Phyllis J., and Bernard L. Witlieb, *The Book of Women's Firsts*. Random House, 1992, pp. 431-32.

1907 ▪ **Annette Kellerman** (1888-1975), an Australian swimmer and actress, appeared on Revere Beach in Boston, Massachusetts, in a one-piece bathing suit. She was one of the first women to appear in public in such an outfit.

Source: Woolum, Janet, *Outstanding Women Athletes: Who They Are and How They Influenced Sports in America*. Phoenix, Arizona: Oryx Press, 1992, p. 25.

1907 ▪ **Dorothy Tyler** (1893-?) was the first female jockey to ride in the United States. Riding her own horse named Blackman, Tyler won a quarter-mile race in her hometown of Joplin, Missouri.

Source: Read, Phyllis J., and Bernard L. Witlieb, *The Book of Women's Firsts*. New York: Random House, 1992, p. 454.

1910 ▪ **Eleonora Sears** (1881-1968), an American athlete, was the first woman to play against men in a polo match. The game took place at Narragansett Pier, Rhode Island, on August 13, 1910. Sears played for two periods riding sidesaddle and two periods astride.

Source: Read, Phyllis J., and Bernard L. Witlieb, *The Book of Women's Firsts*. New York: Random House, 1992, p. 398.

1917 ▪ **Lucy Diggs Slowe** (1885-1937), an African-American athlete, was the first black woman to be a U.S. national champion in any sport. In August 1917 Slowe won the women's singles event at the all-black American Tennis Association championships, held in Druid Hill Park in Baltimore, Maryland.

Source: Smith, Jessie Carney, *Black Firsts: 2000 Years of Extraordinary Achievement*. Detroit: Gale Research Inc., 1994, p. 404.

Women's Bicycle Race

The first women's bicycle race began in Madison Square Garden in New York City on January 6, 1896, much to the distaste of the League of American Wheelmen. By the end of the race at midnight on January 12, all 13 of the original starters had finished. The winner was Frankie Nelson, who rode over 418 miles.

Despite a poor background and persistent health problems, Suzanne Lenglen ranked first in all-time ratings of female tennis players.

1919 ▪ **Suzanne Lenglen** (1899-1938), a French tennis player, revolutionized women's tennis dress when she appeared for a match wearing a short-sleeved, one-piece pleated dress without a petticoat. Lenglen had an impressive tennis career. Despite an underprivileged upbringing and recurring health problems, Lenglen dominated the game in her own country from 1914, when she won the international Clay Court Championship at St.

Cloud, and was the world's best-known amateur tennis star from her first Wimbledon title in 1919 until she turned professional in 1926. Lenglen won the French championship seven times (although she missed the event in 1924 because of jaundice). Lenglen died of pernicious anemia (the failure of the blood to carry oxygen to body organs and tissues) on the eve of Wimbledon in 1938 and was awarded a posthumous Cross of the Légion d'Honneur in France.

Source: Magnusson, Magnus, *Larousse Biographical Dictionary*. Edinburgh: Larousse Kingfisher Chambers, Inc., 1994, p. 882.

An All-Female Auto Race

The first all-female auto race was held on January 12, 1909. Sponsored by the Woman's Motoring Club, all 12 entrants raced from New York City to Philadelphia, returning to New York several days later.

1920 ▪ **Marjorie Voorhies** won the first national tournament for women horseshoe pitchers. (Horseshoe pitching is a game in which a stake is placed in the ground at the end of a stretch of dirt or sand. The object is for players to toss a horseshoe and "ring" the stake.)

Source: Woolum, Janet, *Outstanding Women Athletes: Who They Are and How They Influenced Sports in America*. Phoenix, Arizona: Oryx Press, 1992, p. 26.

1920 ▪ **Aileen Riggin** (1906-), a U.S. athlete, was the first woman to win an Olympic springboard diving event during the first Olympics at which the event was held, in 1920, in Antwerp, Belgium. In 1924 Riggin became the first athlete to win Olympic medals in both swimming and diving events.

Source: O'Neill, Lois Decker, ed., *The Women's Book of World Records and Achievements*. Garden City, New York: Doubleday, 1979, p. 572.

1923 ▪ **Hazel Hotchkiss Wightman** (1886-1974), an American tennis player, established the Wightman Cup, the first international women's tennis competition. Hotchkiss Wightman donated a silver vase, in honor of her husband George Wightman, to the U.S. Lawn Tennis Association as a prize in international women's team tennis. The first match, between the United States and Great Britain, took place in Forest Hills, New York, and was won by Hotchkiss and her partner, Eleanor Goss, for the United States.

Source: Read, Phyllis J., and Bernard L. Witlieb, *The Book of Women's Firsts*. New York: Random House, 1992, p. 481.

Sybil Bauer was the first woman to win an Olympic gold medal in the 100-meter backstroke event.

1924 ▪ **Joyce Wethered** (1901-), an English amateur golfer, was the first woman to win the English Ladies' Golf Championship during five successive years, from 1920 through 1924. Wethered wrote at length about her sport and was known for her intense concentration while playing the game.

Source: Wallechinsky, David, and Irving Wallace, *The People's Almanac.* Garden City, New York: Doubleday, 1975, p. 1186.

1924 ▪ **Sybil Bauer,** an American swimmer, was the first woman to win an Olympic gold medal in the 100-meter backstroke event. Bauer won her medal in Paris, France, the first year in which the backstroke was open to female competitors. When Bauer won this race, she became the first woman to break an existing men's world swimming record, with a time of 1.232 minutes.

Source: O'Neill, Lois Decker, ed., *The Women's Book of World Records and Achievements.* Garden City, New York: Doubleday, 1979, p. 572.

1926 ▪ **Gertrude Ederle** (1906-), an American swimmer, was the first woman to swim the English Channel. She left Cap Gris-Nez, France, on August 6, 1926, and reached Dover, England, 14 hours and 31 minutes later, breaking the previous men's record by one hour and 59 minutes.

Source: Read, Phyllis J., and Bernard L. Witlieb, *The Book of Women's Firsts.* New York: Random House, 1992, pp. 137-38.

1928 ▪ **Lina Radke,** a German runner, was the first woman to win an Olympic gold medal in the 800-meter track and field event, in Amsterdam, the Netherlands, in 1928, the first year in which this event was open to women. The event was subsequently discontinued and not open again to female competitors until 1960, when a Soviet woman named Lyudmila Schevtsova won the event.

Source: O'Neill, Lois Decker, ed., *The Women's Book of World Records and Achievements*. Garden City, New York: Doubleday, 1979, p. 573.

1931 ▪ Lili de Alvarez, a Spanish tennis player, appeared on center court at Wimbledon wearing shorts, the first woman to don such radical attire in the prestigious tennis event.

Source: Woolum, Janet, *Outstanding Women Athletes: Who They Are and How They Influenced Sports in America*. Phoenix, Arizona: Oryx Press, 1992, p. 26.

1935 ▪ Ora Mae Washington (1898-1971), an American tennis player, was the first African-American woman to win seven consecutive titles in the American Tennis Association. This all-black organization held its tournaments at Druid Hill Park in Baltimore, Maryland, beginning in 1917.

Source: Smith, Jessie Carney, *Black Firsts: 2000 Years of Extraordinary Achievement*. Detroit: Gale Research Inc., 1994, p. 404.

1935 ▪ Mary Hirsch became the first licensed trainer of thoroughbred race horses in the United States. In 1937 Hirsch was also the first female trainer of a horse that ran in the Kentucky Derby (a prestigious horse race that makes up one-third of the "Triple Crown." The other two horse races in the "crown" are the Belmont Stakes and the Preakness.)

Source: Read, Phyllis J., and Bernard L. Witlieb, *The Book of Women's Firsts*. New York: Random House, 1992, p. 207.

1935 ▪ Helen Wills Moody (1905-), an American tennis player, was the first person to win the singles event at Wimbledon eight times. She was also the first woman to win 31 titles in the combined tournaments at Wimbledon, Forest Hills, and Paris, France, between 1926 and 1938. Moody retired from the tennis circuit in 1938.

Source: Uglow, Jennifer S., ed., *The Continuum Dictionary of Women's Biography*. New York: Continuum, 1989, pp. 386-87.

AAU Track Meet Held

The Amateur Athletic Union (AAU) sponsored the first major outdoor track and field meet for women at Newark, New Jersey, in 1923. The winners included: 100-meter dash, Frances Rupert (12 seconds); 80-meter hurdles, Hazel Kirk (9.6 seconds); 400-meter relay, the Meadowbrook Club team of Philadelphia (52.4 seconds); high jump, Catherine Wright (4 feet, 7.5 inches); long jump, Helen Dinnehey (15 feet, 4 inches); and discus throw, Babe Wolbert (71 feet, 9.5 inches).

1936 ▪ **Dorothy Dyne Steel** (1884-1965), England's best cro-quet player, was the first woman to win the Open Croquet Championship four times. (Croquet is a lawn game played with wooden mallets.) Steel won the event in 1925, 1933, 1935, and 1936. Only two other women to date have ever won the championship trophy. Steel was also the first player to win the Women's Championship 15 times (between 1919 and

1939) and the first person to win 31 croquet titles in a lifetime of play.

Source: Uglow, Jennifer S., ed., *The Continuum Dictionary of Women's Biography.* New York: Continuum, 1989, p. 515.

1939 ▪ **Gertrude Huntley,** an American schoolteacher, was the first woman to become a champion checkers player. She won a national tournament in 1939 and since that time has been listed as the unofficial U.S. Women's Champion.

Source: O'Neill, Lois Decker, ed., *The Women's Book of World Records and Achievements.* Garden City, New York: Doubleday, 1979, p. 592.

1943 ▪ **Judy Johnson,** an English jockey, rode her horse Lone Gallant to a tenth place finish in a field of 11 horses in a steeplechase event at the Pimlico Racetrack at Baltimore, Maryland. (A steeplechase is a horse race held on a closed course with obstacles such as hedges and fences.) Johnson was the first female steeplechase jockey to race at a major American racetrack.

Source: Woolum, Janet, *Outstanding Women Athletes: Who They Are and How They Influenced Sports in America.* Phoenix, Arizona: Oryx Press, 1992, p. 26.

Swimmer Ann Curtis was the first woman to win the James E. Sullivan Award for sportsmanship.

1944 ▪ **Ann Curtis** (1926-), an American swimmer, was the first woman to win the James E. Sullivan Award of the Amateur Athletic Union (AAU). The award is given to the amateur athlete who best advances the cause of sportsmanship during a given year.

Source: McCullough, Joan, *First of All: Significant "Firsts" by American Women.* New York: Holt, 1980, p. 158.

1946 ▪ **Patty Berg,** an American golfer, defeated Betty Jameson in the final round to win the first U.S. Women's Open golf tournament on September 1, 1946.

Source: Woolum, Janet, *Outstanding Women Athletes: Who They Are and How They Influenced Sports in America.* Phoenix, Arizona: Oryx Press, 1992, p. 27.

Female Ref in the Ring

Belle Martell, an American boxing official, was the first female boxing referee. In 1940 Martell officiated her first match of eight bouts in San Bernardino, California.

1946 ▪ **Mildred "Babe" Didrikson-Zaharias** (1914-1956), an American athlete, became the first three-time winner of the Associated Press poll for "Woman Athlete of the Year" (she also won the award in 1932 and 1945). Didrikson-Zaharias, known especially for her achievements in golf, won more medals and tournaments and set more sports records than any other twentieth-century athlete, male or female. In 1947 she was the first U.S. woman to win the British Ladies Golf Championship in Edinburgh, Scotland.

Source: Parry, Melanie, ed., *Larousse Dictionary of Women.* New York: Larousse Kingfisher Chambers, Inc., 1995, p. 710.

1948 ▪ **Fanny Blankers-Koen** (1918-), a Dutch athlete, was the first woman to win four Olympic gold medals in track events. She won her medals at the Olympic games in London, England, in 1948, coming in first in the 100 meters, 200 meters, 80-meter hurdles, and 4x100 meters relay.

Source: O'Neill, Lois Decker, ed., *The Women's Book of World Records and Achievements.* Garden City, New York: Doubleday, 1979, p. 573.

1948 ▪ **Vicki Manolo Draves** became the first woman to win a gold medal in two diving events at the same Olympics. Draves set this record at the summer Olympics in London, England, in 1948.

Source: Mallon, Bill, and others, *Quest for Gold: The Encyclopedia of American Olympics.* Champaign, Illinois: Human Kinetics, 1984, p. 83.

1948 ▪ **Gretchen Fraser** (1919-), an American skier, became the first woman in the United States to win an Olympic medal in skiing. Fraser earned a silver medal in the women's alpine combined event at the Winter Olympics held in St. Moritz, Switzerland, on February 4, 1948. The next day Fraser earned the first gold medal in skiing awarded to an American skier when she won the special slalom event.

Source: Read, Phyllis J., and Bernard L. Witlieb, *The Book of Women's Firsts.* New York: Random House, 1992, p. 166.

1950 ▪ **Althea Gibson** (1927-), an African-American athlete, broke the color barrier in tennis when she played at the U.S. National Tennis Championship at Forest Hills, New York. On July 6, 1957, Gibson was also the first black female player to win a Wimbledon tennis title in the women's singles event. Later that month, on July 21, Gibson won the first national clay court singles championship,

Fanny Blankers-Koen of Holland was the first woman to win four Olympic gold medals in track events.

First Female Rifle Competition

The first women's annual rifle competition was held in 1952. The Randle Women's International Team Trophy was awarded to the winning 10-woman team in a small-bore rifle match. (The bore is the interior diameter of the gun barrel.) Sponsored by the National Rifle Association, the U.S. women's team won for the first 13 years before the British triumphed in 1965.

becoming the first black woman to win a major U.S. tennis title.

Source: Parry, Melanie, ed., *Larousse Dictionary of Women.* New York: Larousse Kingfisher Chambers, Inc., 1995, p. 265.

1950 ▪ Florence Chadwick (1919-1995), an American swimmer, was the first woman to swim both ways across the English Channel. She swam from France to England in 1950, setting a new record of 13 hours and 20 minutes; the next year, she swam the more difficult route from England to France. Chadwick swam the English Channel four times and the Catalina Channel between California and Catalina Island three times.

Source: Uglow, Jennifer S., ed., *The Continuum Dictionary of Women's Biography.* New York: Continuum, 1989, p. 117.

1953 ▪ Tenley Albright (1935-), an ice skater, was the first American woman to win the World Figure Skating Championship. Three years later, on February 2, 1956, Albright won the gold medal in figure skating at the winter Olympic Games in Cortina, Italy—the first American woman to do so. At the time of her wins, Albright was a premedical student; she eventually became a successful physician.

Source: Woolum, Janet, *Outstanding Women Athletes: Who They Are and How They Influenced Sports in America.* Phoenix, Arizona: Oryx Press, 1992, p. 27.

1953 ▪ Maureen Connolly (1934-1969), an American tennis player, became the first woman to win the grand slam of tennis in 1953. After winning the Wimbledon Championship in England in 1952, Connolly went on to win the Australian, French, and U.S. tennis championships, thus achieving the four triumphs that comprise the "grand slam" in this sport.

Source: Wallechinsky, David, and Irving Wallace, *The People's Almanac.* Garden City, New York: Doubleday, 1975, p. 1188.

1957 ▪ Patricia McCormick was the first American female bullfighter. She first entered the bullfighting arena in Cuidad Juarez, Mexico, on January 25, 1957.

Source: Woolum, Janet, *Outstanding Women Athletes: Who They Are and How They Influenced Sports in America.* Phoenix, Arizona: Oryx Press, 1992, p. 27.

Tenley Albright was the first American woman to win the World Figure Skating Championship.

Romanian athlete Iolanda Balas was the first woman to clear six feet in the high jump.

1958 ▪ **Iolanda Balas** (1936-), a Romanian athlete, was the first woman to clear six feet in the high jump. Between 1956 and 1961, Balas set 14 world high-jump records. In 1964 she was also the first athlete to win two Olympic gold medals in the high jump event. Balas won gold medals at both the 1960 Olympics in Rome, Italy, and the 1964 Olympics in Tokyo, Japan, breaking the current Olympic record each time.

Source: Uglow, Jennifer S., ed., *The Continuum Dictionary of Women's Biography.* New York: Continuum, 1989, p. 44.

1960 ▪ Wilma Rudolph (1940-1994), an American athlete, was the first female runner to win three gold medals at a single Olympic games. At the 1960 Olympics in Rome, Italy, she won the 100-meter and the 200-meter events, and was on the winning team for the 400-meter relay. Named to the Women's Sports Hall of Fame in 1980, Rudolph overcame much hardship to become a great athlete. As a child she was afflicted by poliomyelitis (also called polio; a viral disease that can lead to swelling around the spinal cord and paralysis), and doctors predicted she would never walk again. By the time she was in high school, however, Rudolph was a star basketball player. Rudolph became a runner at the age of 16 and won a bronze medal at the 1956 Olympics in Melbourne, Australia. She was inducted into the National Women's Hall of Fame in 1994.

Source: Parry, Melanie, ed., *Larousse Dictionary of Women.* New York: Larousse Kingfisher Chambers, Inc., 1995, p. 571.

1964 ▪ Lydia Skoblikova (1939-), a schoolteacher from Siberia, was the first athlete (male or female) to win four gold medals in a single winter Olympics. Skoblikova achieved this accomplishment in 1964 during the games held at Innsbruck, Austria. Her gold medals were won in four speed skating events: 500-meters, 1,000 meters, 1,500 meters, and 3,000 meters. She won the gold medal in both the 1,500 and 3,000 meters speed skating events at the 1960 Winter Olympics in Squaw Valley, California.

Source: O'Neill, Lois Decker, ed., *The Women's Book of World Records and Achievements.* Garden City, New York: Doubleday, 1979, p. 574.

1964 ▪ Dawn Fraser (1937-), an Australian swimmer, was the first competitor to win the 100-meter freestyle gold medal at the Olympic games in three successive games: in 1956, 1960, and 1964. In the late 1950s she was also the first woman to swim 100 meters and 110 yards in under a minute.

Source: Uglow, Jennifer S., ed., *The Continuum Dictionary of Women's Biography.* New York: Continuum, 1989, p. 213.

1964 ▪ **Larissa Latynina** (1935-), a Russian gymnast, was the first person to win 18 medals during the course of three Olympic Games. In the games played in 1956, 1960, and 1964, she won more Olympic medals than anyone else in any sport: six individual golds, three golds as a team member, five silver, and three bronze medals. At the end of her 13-year career, Latynina had won 24 titles in Olympic, World, and European championship competitions. Latynina retired in 1966.

Source: Uglow, Jennifer S., ed., *The Continuum Dictionary of Women's Biography.* New York: Continuum, 1989, p. 313.

1967 ▪ **Katherine Switzer** (1947-), an American runner, became the first woman to register to run in the Boston Marathon. Since the race was closed to women, she registered unofficially as "K. Switzer." Published photographs of an official trying to remove her number created an outpouring of public opinion. Switzer competed officially in the marathon when it was finally opened to women in 1972.

The first woman to compete unofficially in the Boston Marathon was Roberta Gibb (Bingay) (1942-). On April 19, 1966, Gibb hid in the bushes near the starting line and leapt into the pack of male runners just after the official start. She wore a hooded sweatshirt to disguise her appearance because women were not allowed to run in the race. Gibb finished ahead of 415 men—over half the racing field—but officials denied that a woman had run that day.

Source: McCullough, Joan, *First of All: Significant "Firsts" by American Women.* New York: Holt, 1980, p. 145.

1967 ▪ **Otrum Enderlein,** a German athlete, was the first woman to hold four luge titles. (A luge is a small sled in which the rider lies down to steer.) She earned her first title at the 1964 Winter Olympics in Innsbruck, Austria, and the others between that date and 1967. When Enderlein won the Olympic gold medal in 1964, she became the first woman to do so (this event was open to female competitors for the first time that year).

Source: O'Neill, Lois Decker, ed., *The Women's Book of World Records and Achievements.* Garden City, New York: Doubleday, 1979, pp. 564-65.

1968 ▪ **Vera Caslavska-Oklozil** (1942-), a Czech athlete, was the first woman to win seven individual gold Olympic medals in gymnastics. She won three at the 1964 Olympic games and four more at the games in 1968.

Source: O'Neill, Lois Decker, ed., *The Women's Book of World Records and Achievements.* Garden City, New York: Doubleday, 1979, p. 562.

1968 ▪ **Althea Gibson** (1927-), a U.S. tennis player, was the first African American inducted into the International Tennis Hall of Fame. Gibson's career in sports includes a number of firsts: she was the first African American invited to play in the American Lawn Tennis Association championships, in 1950; she was the first African American to win at Wimbledon, in 1957; and she was the first African-American athlete to win a major U.S. national championship when she played at Forest Hills, New York, also in 1957. Gibson published her autobiography, *I Always Wanted to be Somebody,* the following year. In 1991 Gibson became the first black woman to receive the Theodore Roosevelt Award from the National Collegiate Athletic Association (NCAA).

Source: Parry, Melanie, ed., *Larousse Dictionary of Women.* New York: Larousse Kingfisher Chambers, Inc., 1995, p. 265.

1969 ▪ **Barbara Jo Rubin** (1949-), an American jockey, was the first female jockey to win a regular parimutuel thoroughbred horse race. (In a parimutuel race the first three winning riders share money that has been collected from bets.) In January 1969 she rode the horse Fly Away at Hobby Horse Hall racetrack in Nassau, the Bahamas. The following month Rubin became the first woman jockey to win a race at a U.S. thoroughbred track (a track that holds races for horses specially bred for racing). Rubin rode her horse Cohesion to victory at Charles Town, West Virginia.

Source: Read, Phyllis J., and Bernard L. Witlieb, *The Book of Women's Firsts.* New York: Random House, 1992, pp. 383-84.

1970 ▪ **Cathy Rigby** (1952-), an American gymnast, was the first United States athlete to win a medal at the World Gym-

Chi Cheng Set Record

On June 13, 1970, Chi Cheng (1944-), a Taiwanese runner, was the first woman to run one hundred yards in 10 seconds in an official competition.

nastics Championships. In 1970 she won a silver medal for her performance on the balance beam (a narrow wooden beam, supported 4 feet above the floor, on which the gymnast performs). Two years later Rigby won the American Amateur Athletic Union women's gymnastics all-around title. A popular public figure, she retired in 1973 to pursue successful business and acting careers.

Source: O'Neill, Lois Decker, ed., *The Women's Book of World Records and Achievements.* Garden City, New York: Doubleday, 1979, p. 562.

1970 ▪ Diane Crump (1949-), an American jockey, was the first female jockey to ride in the Kentucky Derby in Louisville, Kentucky. Crump rode her horse Fathom in the Churchill Downs racing classic, placing fifteenth in a field of 17. She rode her first mount to a tenth-place finish at a Hialeah, Florida, race track on February 7, 1969. Crump later went on to a lucrative career as a jockey and a horse trainer.

Source: Read, Phyllis J., and Bernard L. Witlieb, *The Book of Women's Firsts.* New York: Random House, 1992, pp. 108-09.

1972 ▪ Olga Korbut (1955-), a Russian gymnast, was the first person to demonstrate a backwards somersault on uneven parallel bars in competition. (The uneven parallel bars are two wooden bars, supported horizontally above the floor at different heights, on which a gymnast performs.) Korbut accomplished this feat during the Olympic Games in Munich, Germany, in 1972. Korbut also became the first and only female to do a back flip on the balance beam during these games, at which she won three gold medals. (The balance beam is a narrow wooden beam, supported 4 feet above the floor, on which the gymnast performs.) She electrified audiences around the world with her performance, sparking increased interest in women's gymnastics. By 1976, however, Korbut had grown weary of the sport. She retired and married a popular Russian singer, Leonid Bartkevich.

Source: O'Neill, Lois Decker, ed., *The Women's Book of World Records and Achievements.* Garden City, New York: Doubleday, 1979, pp. 561-62.

1972 ▪ **Doreen Wilber** (1930-), an American archer, was the first woman to win the Olympic individual archery championship in Munich, West Germany. (Archery is the sport of shooting a bow and arrow in competition.) This was the first year the event was held. A housewife from Jefferson, Iowa, Wilber set a world record of 2,424 points.

Source: Read, Phyllis J., and Bernard L. Witlieb, *The Book of Women's Firsts.* New York: Random House, 1992, pp. 481-82.

1972 ▪ **Nina Kuscik,** an American runner, was the first official female finisher in the 76th Boston Marathon. The 1972 race marked the first year that the event was officially open to women. Kuscik and eight other women took to the Boston streets as official registrants, even though women had been running unofficially since 1966. Kuscik finished with a time of 3 hours, 8 minutes, 58 seconds, ahead of at least two-thirds of the men.

Source: McCullough, Joan, *First of All: Significant "Firsts" by American Women.* New York: Holt, p. 147.

1973 ▪ **Dacie Schileru,** an American swimmer, was the first woman to compete in a National Collegiate Athletic Association (NCAA) event. As a result of Title IX legislation passed by the U.S. Congress in 1972, 1973 was the first year women were declared eligible for competition sponsored by the NCAA. (Outlawing sex discrimination, Title IX allowed women equal access and opportunities in education, which includes sports.) Schileru qualified for diving competition in the swimming championships.

Source: Read, Phyllis J., and Bernard L. Witlieb, *The Book of Women's Firsts.* New York: Random House, 1992, p. 394.

1973 ▪ **Robyn Smith** (1943-), an American jockey, became the first female jockey to win a stake race. (In a stake race, at least part of the prize money consists of entry fees paid by the owners of the race horses.) Smith rode North Sea to victory in the $27,450 Paumanauk Handicap at Aqueduct Raceway, Queens, New York, on March 1, 1973. From 1972 to 1978 she was the only American jockey with international standing (she ranked seventh). Smith is also known for her marriage, in 1980, to the dancer and movie star Fred Astaire (1899-1987).

Source: Parry, Melanie, ed., *Larousse Dictionary of Women.* New York: Larousse Kingfisher Chambers, Inc., 1995, p. 606.

1974 ▪ **Julie Meissner,** a ski instructor and racing coach from Idaho, was the first woman to win the all-around freestyle event at the Women's International Ballet and Freestyle Ski Competition. She achieved this distinction the first time the event was held, in 1974.

Source: O'Neill, Lois Decker, ed., *The Women's Book of World Records and Achievements.* Garden City, New York: Doubleday, 1979, p. 566.

1974 ▪ **Rika Marcus,** a British bridge player, was the first woman to attain the rank of World Bridge Federation "Grand-master." (Bridge is a card game.) A competitor in international play since 1935, Marcus had won 12 international championships by 1974, a women's record.

Source: O'Neill, Lois Decker, ed., *The Women's Book of World Records and Achievements.* Garden City, New York: Doubleday, 1979, p. 592.

1974 ▪ **Kazuko Sawamatsu** (1951-), a Japanese tennis player, became the first female tennis player in Japan to turn professional. She achieved this distinction when she won a title at the prestigious Wimbledon Championships in England 1974. In her own country Sawamatsu had won 192 consecutive tournaments, a world record.

Source: O'Neill, Lois Decker, ed., *The Women's Book of World Records and Achievements.* Garden City, New York: Doubleday, 1979, p. 583.

1975 ▪ **Marion Bermudez** (1952-), an American boxer, was the first woman to compete successfully in the previously all-male Golden Gloves Boxing Tournament, held in 1975 in Mexico City, Mexico. She won her first match against a man after only seven practice rounds the week before. Bermudez was also a national karate champion; she competed against men in that sport, as well.

Source: O'Neill, Lois Decker, ed., *The Women's Book of World Records and Achievements.* Garden City, New York: Doubleday, 1979, p. 559.

1975 ▪ **Ludmilla Tourisheva,** a Russian athlete, became the only female gymnast to hold all the gold medals in both European and world championships at one time.

Source: O'Neill, Lois Decker, ed., *The Women's Book of World Records and Achievements.* Garden City, New York: Doubleday, 1979, p. 562.

1975 ▪ **Margaret Murdock,** an American rifle champion, was the first woman to win a gold medal in the overall shooting events at the Pan American Games. All of Murdock's competitors were male. The following year she won a silver medal in the Olympic games in Montreal, Canada.

Source: O'Neill, Lois Decker, ed., *The Women's Book of World Records and Achievements.* Garden City, New York: Doubleday, 1979, p. 565.

1975 ▪ **Marion May,** an American runner, was the first woman marathon runner to win in an open competition against men. The first time she had ever competed in an official marathon, May defeated 53 men in the Fairbanks, Alaska, Midnight Sun Marathon on June 14, 1975.

Source: McCullough, Joan, *First of All: Significant "Firsts" by American Women.* New York: Holt, p. 145.

1975 ▪ **Margo Oberg** (1955-), an American surfer, was the first woman to win the Hang Ten International Surfing Competition. Held in Malibu, California, in 1975, the Hang Ten meet was the first professional surfing contest held for women. Oberg was only 12 years old when she won her first surfing title at the Menehune Competition at La Jolla, California.

Source: O'Neill, Lois Decker, ed., *The Women's Book of World Records and Achievements.* Garden City, New York: Doubleday, 1979, p. 585.

1975 ▪ **Diana Nyad** (1949-), an American athlete, was the first person to swim across Lake Ontario. The 32-mile non-stop journey took the marathon swimmer 20 hours. That same year, Nyad swam around Manhattan Island in 7 hours, 57 minutes, breaking a record set by Bryan Somers almost 50 years earlier.

Source: O'Neill, Lois Decker, ed., *The Women's Book of World Records and Achievements.* Garden City, New York: Doubleday, 1979, p. 586.

1976 ▪ **Sally Little,** a South African athlete, was the first woman to win the Women's International Golf Tournament, offered for the first time in 1976. This victory was her first in six years of professional competition.

Source: O'Neill, Lois Decker, ed., *The Women's Book of World Records and Achievements.* Garden City, New York: Doubleday, 1979, p. 561.

1976 ▪ **Natalie Dunn** (1956-), an American roller skater, was the first U.S. athlete to win the world title in figure roller skating, in Rome, Italy, in 1976. She successfully defended her crown the following year in Montreal, Canada. Dunn won her first event at the age of seven and in 1972 took the national women's singles title.

Source: Read, Phyllis J., and Bernard L. Witlieb, *The Book of Women's Firsts.* New York: Random House, 1992, p. 127.

1976 ▪ **Ivanka Khristova** was the first Bulgarian woman to win an Olympic gold medal in a track and field event. At the summer Olympic games in Montreal, Canada, in 1976, Khristova came in first in the shot put, setting a world record.

Source: O'Neill, Lois Decker, ed., *The Women's Book of World Records and Achievements.* Garden City, New York: Doubleday, 1979, p. 579.

1977 ▪ **Lucy Giovinco,** an American bowler, was the first U.S. woman to win the Women's Bowling World Cup Competition. In 1977, she averaged 178 points per game and bowled a remarkable 620 in a three-game round to beat her opponent by 116 points.

Source: O'Neill, Lois Decker, ed., *The Women's Book of World Records and Achievements.* Garden City, New York: Doubleday, 1979, p. 558.

1977 ▪ **Eva Shain** (1929-), an American boxing official, was the first woman to judge a world heavyweight boxing match. She officiated in the Muhammad Ali-Ernie Shavers fight at Madison Square Garden in New York City on September 29, 1977.

Source: Read, Phyllis J., and Bernard L. Witlieb, *The Book of Women's Firsts.* New York: Random House, 1992, p. 404.

1977 ▪ **Jan Todd,** an American weight lifter, became the first woman to lift more than one thousand pounds in three power lifts. Todd bench pressed 176 pounds, deadlifted 441 pounds, and lifted 424 pounds from a squat. (Bench pressing involves lifting weights while lying on a bench. Deadlifting is lifting a weight from the floor to hip level.)

Source: Woolum, Janet, *Outstanding Women Athletes: Who They Are and How They Influenced Sports in America.* Phoenix, Arizona: Oryx Press, 1992, p. 29.

1978 ▪ **Nancy Lopez** (1957-), an American golfer, became the first woman to win five straight Ladies Professional Golf Association (LPGA) tournaments. She accomplished this feat when she won her fifth tournament in 1978. She won the LPGA tournament again in 1985 and 1989. In 1985 Lopez set a record for prize money by becoming the first woman to earn over $416,000.

Source: Read, Phyllis J., and Bernard L. Witlieb, *The Book of Women's Firsts.* New York: Random House, 1992, pp. 258-59.

In 1985 golfer Nancy Lopez set a record for prize money by becoming the first woman to earn over $416,000.

1980s ▪ **Martina Navratilova** (1957-), a Czechoslovakian-born American tennis player, was the first athlete to win over nine million dollars in prize money. She defected (left her native country) to the United States while competing at the U.S. Open in New York in 1975. Navratilova is known internationally for her stature as a tennis star and for her outspoken views on lesbian issues. In 1983 she established the Martina Foundation with a large portion of her prize money. The organization is devoted to helping underprivileged children throughout the world.

Source: Uglow, Jennifer S., ed., *The Continuum Dictionary of Women's Biography.* New York: Continuum, 1989, p. 397.

1980 ▪ **Pamela Shuttleworth** was the first female caddie for the Professional Golf Association (PGA). (A caddie assists a golfer by carrying clubs.) The PGA allowed female caddies in the U.S. Open at the Baltusrol Golf Club in Springfield, New Jersey, in June 1980. Shuttleworth caddied for professional golfer Jim Dent.

Source: Woolum, Janet, *Outstanding Women Athletes: Who They Are and How They Influenced Sports in America.* Phoenix, Arizona: Oryx Press, 1992, p. 30.

1982 ▪ **Marita Koch** (1957-), a German track star, was voted the best female athlete in the world three times: in 1978, 1979, and 1982. She was also the first woman to break the record of 49 seconds for 400 meters and 22 seconds for 200 meters. During her career she has set 16 world records outdoors and 14 world bests indoors.

Source: Uglow, Jennifer S., ed., *The Continuum Dictionary of Women's Biography.* New York: Continuum, 1989, p. 302.

1984 ▪ **Billie Jean King** (1943-), an American tennis champion, became the first female commissioner of a professional sport. When King accepted the governorship of World Team Tennis, she had already received numerous honors during her career as a tennis champion. Inducted into the International Tennis Hall of Fame in 1987, King was named by *Life* magazine as one of the "100 most important Americans of the twentieth century." She joined baseball stars Babe Ruth and Jackie Robinson and boxing champion Muhammad Ali as the only athletes on the list.

Source: *Working Woman,* November-December, 1996, p. 67.

1984 ▪ **Mary Lou Retton** (1968-), an American athlete, was the first U.S. female gymnast to win a gold medal at the Olympics. She set this record at the 1984 Olympic Games in Los Angeles, California. Retton was the most decorated U.S. athlete at these games and went on to a career in commercials and small parts in films. She soon became the first woman to appear on the front of a "Wheaties" cereal box, a traditional showcase for male athletes.

Source: Parry, Melanie, ed., *Larousse Dictionary of Women.* New York: Larousse Kingfisher Chambers, Inc., 1995, p. 554.

1985 ▪ **Ingrid Kristiansen** (1956-), a Norwegian runner, was the first person to set world records at 5,000 meters (in 1981 and 1984), at 10,000 meters (in 1985), and in the marathon (in 1985). She was undefeated in 1986, her best running year.

Source: Uglow, Jennifer S., ed., *The Continuum Dictionary of Women's Biography.* New York: Continuum, 1989, p. 306.

In 1987 famed tennis player Billie Jean King was named by Life magazine as one of the "100 most important Americans of the twentieth century."

Mary Lou Retton was the first U.S. female gymnast to win a gold medal at the Olympics.

1986 ▪ Ayako Okamoto (1951-), an outstanding Japanese professional golfer, was the first woman to score 17 under par at a U.S. golf tournament (the Elizabeth Arden Classic). This feat earned Okamoto a place in the *Guinness Book of Records.*

Source: Uglow, Jennifer S. ed., *The Continuum Dictionary of Women's Biography.* New York: Continuum, 1989, p. 411.

1990 ▪ Juli Inkster (1960-), an American golfer, became the first woman to win the only professional golf tournament in the world in which women and men competed as equals. Inkster parred (achieved the standard score) on the eighteenth hole of the Spaulding Invitational Pro-Am at Pebble Beach, California. She won a one-stroke victory over Professional Golf Association (PGA) tour member Mark Brooks.

Source: Woolum, Janet, *Outstanding Women Athletes: Who They Are and How They Influenced Sports in America.* Phoenix, Arizona: Oryx Press, 1992, p. 31.

1991 ▪ **Judit Polgar** (1976-), a Hungarian chess player, became the youngest grand master. (A grand master is a chess player who consistently scores high in international competition.) She was given the title by the International Chess Federation. Polgar was only the fourth woman to hold this rank (Polgar's sister Zsuzsu was one of the other women). At age 15, Polgar was the youngest person—male or female—to become a grand master. In February of 1993, Polgar defeated former world chess champion Boris Spassky in a 10-game exhibition match staged in Budapest, Hungary. She won $110,000 for her efforts.

Source: *People Weekly,* August 10, 1992.

Female Triathalon

The first "women only" triathlon was held in Long Beach, California, in June of 1990. More than 2,000 women competed in the three events, which included an ocean swim, a bicycle race, and a marathon run.

1993 ▪ **Julie Krone** (1964-), an American jockey, was the first woman to win a Triple Crown event. Riding the horse Colonial Affair, Krone came in first at New York's Belmont Stakes. (The Triple Crown is an unofficial title given to the rider whose horse wins the three major thoroughbred races: the Kentucky Derby, the Preakness, and the Belmont Stakes.) Two years earlier, Krone was the first woman to ride at Belmont.

Source: Parry, Melanie, ed., *Larousse Dictionary of Women.* New York: Larousse Kingfisher Chambers, Inc., 1995, p. 376.

1994 ▪ **Bonnie Blair** (1964-), an American speed skater, became the first U.S. woman to win five gold medals at a winter Olympics. Among her wins was the 1,000 meter speed skating race. After winning an additional bronze medal during the 1994 Olympiad, Blair became the United States' most successful winter Olympian.

Source: *The New York Times,* February 24, 1994.

1996 ▪ **Penelope Heyns,** a South African swimmer, set an Olympic record with her first-place performance in the 100-meter breaststroke event with a time of 1 minute, 7.02 seconds

Swimmer Set Record

Amy Van Dyken, an American swimmer, set a U.S. Olympic record when she earned four gold medals at the 1996 Olympics in Atlanta, Georgia. No other American woman has ever achieved this feat in a single Olympic games. Seventeen other women have won three gold medals.

at the 1996 Olympics in Atlanta, Georgia. Setting both a world record and an Olympic record, Heyns also earned her country's first Olympic gold medal in forty-four years.

Source: *Sports Illustrated.* July 29, 1996, p. 45.

1996 ▪ Deon Hemmings, a Jamaican runner, became the first Jamaican woman to win an Olympic gold medal. Setting a new Olympic record, Hemmings placed first in the women's 400-meter hurdles race at the 1996 Olympics in Atlanta, Georgia. Her time was 52.82 seconds.

Source: Famighetti, Robert, ed., *The World Almanac and Book of Facts.* Mahwah, New Jersey: World Almanac, 1997, p. 852.

1996 ▪ Merlene Ottey, a Jamaican runner, placed second, earning a silver medal, and thereby made Olympic history by becoming the first runner ever to make the final in five Olympic games in the same event. She placed second in the final 200-meter event at the 1996 Olympics in Atlanta, Georgia. She also won bronze medals, in 1980, 1984, and 1990.

Source: *Sports Illustrated.* August 5, 1996, p. 46.

1996 ▪ Heli Rantanen, a Finnish athlete, became the first-ever Finnish female Olympic gold medalist. She won a gold medal in the women's javelin event at the 1996 Olympics in Atlanta, Georgia. Rantanen threw the javelin 67.94 meters to place first in the competition.

Source: Famighetti, Robert, ed., *The World Almanac and Book of Facts.* Mahwah, New Jersey: World Almanac, 1997, p. 852.

1996 ▪ Stefka Kostadinova, a Bulgarian track and field athlete, set a new Olympic record by clearing a height of 2.05 meters in the women's high jump event at the 1996 Olympics in Atlanta, Georgia.

Source: Famighetti, Robert, ed., *The World Almanac and Book of Facts.* Mahwah, New Jersey: World Almanac, 1997, p. 852.

1996 ▪ **Dominique Dawes** (1976-), an American gymnast, became the first African-American gymnast to win an individual Olympic event medal. She earned a bronze medal for her floor routine at the 1996 Olympics in Atlanta, Georgia. Dawes was a member of the gold medal-winning U.S. women's gymnastic team. A four-time world gymnastics championships medalist, she also won the all-around title and all four event titles at the 1994 Coca-Cola National Championships. Dawes was the first gymnast to accomplish this feat since American gymnast Joyce Tanac Schroeder won the all-around and all four events at the 1966 Olympics. Dawes was also a finalist for the 1994 Sullivan Awards, an honor given to the top amateur athlete in the United States.

Source: *The New York Times.* July 28, 1996.

1996 ▪ **Ghada Shouaa,** an athlete from the Syrian Arab Republic, was the first Syrian athlete to win an Olympic medal in track and field. She won a gold medal in the women's heptathlon (seven track and field events) at the 1996 Olympics in Atlanta, Georgia. Breaking the Syrian national record in two of the events, Shouaa was only the second athlete from her country to win a gold medal.

Source: Famighetti, Robert, ed., *The World Almanac and Book of Facts.* Mahwah, New Jersey: World Almanac, 1997, p. 852.

1997 ▪ **Susie Maroney** (1975-), an Australian swimmer, became the first woman to swim the Straits of Florida. Maroney swam 112-miles from Havana, Cuba, to Key West, Florida, in 24 hours. After being diagnosed as having asthma at age three, she began swimming to strengthen her lungs. Maroney has crossed the English Channel twice, and she set the record for swimming the longest distance in 24 hours. She accomplished this feat in a pool.

Source: *The Tampa Tribune,* May 13, 1997.

Team Sports

1867 ▪ The first women's baseball team was organized in Philadelphia, Pennsylvania. Called the "Dolly Vardens," the team players shocked their audiences by appearing in red dresses that were, for the time, immodestly short—well above the ankle. The team ball was made of yarn.

Source: McCullough, Joan, *First of All: Significant "Firsts" by American Women.* New York: Holt, 1980, p. 131.

1875 ▪ The first women's crew rowing team was introduced at Wellesley College in Massachusetts. The row boats at that time were large enough to accommodate ten women in full skirts. By the 1940s, women's crew had grown into a serious sport at many women's colleges.

Source: McCullough, Joan, *First of All: Significant "Firsts" by American Women.* New York: Holt, 1980, p. 136.

1892 ▪ **Senda Berenson** (1868-1954), an American physical education instructor, was the first woman to introduce basketball at a woman's college. Berenson was the director of physical education at Smith College in Northampton, Massachusetts, where she organized a team and arranged to play several intercollegiate games. The first women's intercollegiate basketball game took place at the Armory Hall in San Francisco between Stanford and the University of California at Berkeley on April 4, 1896. Stanford won the contest.

Source: Read, Phyllis J., and Bernard L. Witlieb, *The Book of Women's Firsts.* New York: Random House, 1992, pp. 41-42.

1901 ▪ **Constance Applebee** (1883-1981), an English physical education instructor, introduced the sport of field hockey in the United States. While studying at Harvard University in 1901, Applebee suggested that field hockey be made part of the track and field sport course. The first game was played with ice hockey sticks on a concrete yard outside the Harvard gym.

Source: Uglow, Jennifer S., ed., *The Continuum Dictionary of Women's Biography.* New York: Continuum, 1989, p. 24.

1916 ▪ Forty women organized the Woman's National Bowling Association (now the Women's International Bowling Congress) on November 29, 1916, in St. Louis, Missouri. The association is the largest sports organization for women in the world. Its founders included Ellen Kelly, Gertrude Dornblasser, and Catherine Menne. The first official women's bowling tournament was held in 1917. The Progress team of St. Louis, Missouri, won the first team championship, and Mrs. A. J. Koester, also of St. Louis, won the all-events title.

Source: Read, Phyllis J., and Bernard L. Witlieb, *The Book of Women's Firsts*. New York: Random House, 1992, p. 63.

1922 ▪ The U.S. Field Hockey Association was the first organization to establish standards for women field hockey players in the United States. When the U.S. sent its first field hockey team to the Olympics in 1984, the players won a bronze medal.

Source: Read, Phyllis J., and Bernard L. Witlieb, *The Book of Women's Firsts*. New York: Random House, 1992, p. 209.

1931 ▪ **Verne Beatrice Mitchell,** an American athlete professionally known as "Miss Jack Mitchell," became the first woman to play in major league baseball. She was signed to pitch by the Chattanooga (Tennessee) Lookouts on April 1, 1931, when she was only 17 years old. In her first trip to the mound, in an exhibition game with the New York Yankees on April 3, 1931, she struck out two legends: Babe Ruth and Lou Gehrig.

Source: McCullough, Joan, *First of All: Significant "Firsts" by American Women*. New York: Holt, 1980, p. 130.

1943 ▪ The first professional women's baseball leagues were formed in the early 1940s when male major league team players went off to fight in World War II (1939-1945). In 1943 Philip Wrigley formed the All American Girls Baseball League in Chicago, an organization made up of four teams of women softball players. The teams played high-caliber games that drew many fans; after the war, however, the female players returned to amateur softball.

Source: McCullough, Joan, *First of All: Significant "Firsts" by American Women*. New York: Holt, 1980, p. 131.

First "Ladies' Day"

The New York Gothams baseball team held the first "Ladies' Day" on June 17, 1883, allowing women into baseball parks either at a reduced rate or free of charge, signaling the acceptance of women spectators at public sporting events.

Kallio Started Association

Elin Kallio (1859-1927), a Finnish educator, founded the first athletic association for women in northern Europe. Kallio, who helped to popularize gymnastics in Finland, devoted her life to teaching athletics and to writing books about sports.

1947 The U. S. Women's Curling Association was founded in Milwaukee, Wisconsin, on October 23, 1947. (Curling is a game in which two teams, each with four players, slide stones across an ice surface toward a target circle in the center.)

Source: Woolum, Janet, *Outstanding Women Athletes: Who They Are and How They Influenced Sports in America.* Phoenix, Arizona: Oryx Press, 1992, p. 27.

1970 ▪ Pat Palinkas, an American athlete, was the first woman to play in a professional football game. Palinkas signed a contract with the Orlando, Florida, Panthers in the Atlantic Coast Professional Football League. She held the ball for the point-after-touchdown kicks during a game on August 15, 1970.

Source: Woolum, Janet, *Outstanding Women Athletes: Who They Are and How They Influenced Sports in America.* Phoenix, Arizona: Oryx Press, 1992, p. 28.

1972 ▪ The Soviet women's volleyball team was the first female volleyball team to win three consecutive Olympic gold medals. The women achieved this record at the 1976 Olympic Games in Montreal, Canada, after having won in 1972 at Munich, West Germany, and in 1968 at Mexico City, Mexico. The team was also the first to win a total of six championship titles—in 1952, 1956, 1960, 1968, 1970, and 1973.

Source: Wallechinsky, David, *The Complete Book of the Olympics.* New York: Penguin Books, 1984, pp. 504-05.

1972 ▪ Berenice Gera, an American athletic official, became the first female umpire in professional baseball. Gera officiated at games in the Class "A" New York-Penn (minor) League. In June of 1972, she took the field in a game between two minor league teams, the Auburn Phillies and the Geneva Rangers. This was only game she called, however, due to severe criticism both before and during her debut. Gera quit and took her baseball knowledge to the New York Mets front office.

Source: McCullough, Joan, *First of All: Significant "Firsts" by American Women.* New York: Holt, 1980, p. 161.

1973 ▪ **Carolyn King,** a baseball player, was the defendant in the first lawsuit challenging Little League Baseball's "no girls" rule. The suit was filed on King's behalf in Detroit, Michigan, on June 28, 1973. Detroit courts dismissed the motion, but after stories about the case appeared in newspapers all over the country, similar lawsuits followed. Little League baseball eventually announced that its teams would be open to girls.

On September 7, 1973, the national organization signed an order agreeing to ban sex discrimination. Girls were officially permitted to play in Little League baseball after President Gerald Ford (served in office 1974-1977) signed legislation that opened the organization to children of both sexes on December 26, 1973.

Source: Read, Phyllis J., and Bernard L. Witlieb, *The Book of Women's Firsts.* New York: Random House, 1992, p. 256.

Women's Football League

The first women's professional football league was founded in the United States in 1974. The league included 10 teams, all coached by men, that played 10 games each year. Every player earned $25 per game.

1975 ▪ **Mary Jo Peppler** (1944-), an American volleyball player, was the first woman to win the volleyball Superstars competition. Peppler was voted outstanding volleyball player in the world at the 1970 International Games in Bulgaria, and served as a member of the U.S. Olympic team in 1968.

Source: O'Neill, Lois Decker, ed., *The Women's Book of World Records and Achievements.* Garden City, New York: Doubleday, 1979, p. 570.

1976 ▪ **Inna Ryskal** (1944-), a Russian athlete, was the first woman to win four Olympic medals in volleyball. She won a silver medal at the 1964 Summer Olympic Games in Tokyo, Japan, and gold medals in 1968 (at Mexico City, Mexico), 1972 (at Munich, West Germany), and 1976 (Montreal, Canada).

Source: O'Neill, Lois Decker, ed., *The Women's Book of World Records and Achievements.* Garden City, New York: Doubleday, 1979, p. 570.

1976 ▪ The Soviet women's handball team was the first handball team to win an Olympic gold medal, in Montreal, Canada. This was the first time handball was officially offered as an event and the first year in which this event was open to female competitors.

Source: O'Neill, Lois Decker, ed., *The Women's Book of World Records and Achievements.* Garden City, New York: Doubleday, 1979, pp. 568, 572.

1976 ▪ The Connecticut Falcons were the first women's softball team to win the women's World Series championship title. This team beat the San Jose Sunbirds during the first women's World Series, held in 1976.

Source: O'Neill, Lois Decker, ed., *The Women's Book of World Records and Achievements.* Garden City, New York: Doubleday, 1979, p. 569.

1976 ▪ **Uliana Semenova,** a Russian basketball player, was captain of the first team to win an Olympic gold medal in basketball. The Soviet team achieved this record in Montreal, Canada, in 1976, the first year basketball became an official Olympic event. This virtually unchallenged team went on to win the Women's World Championship for the sixth consecutive time in 1976.

Source: O'Neill, Lois Decker, ed., *The Women's Book of World Records and Achievements.* Garden City, New York: Doubleday, 1979, p. 567.

1978 ▪ The first game of the Women's Professional Basketball League took place between the Chicago Hustle and the Milwaukee Does on December 9, 1978.

Source: Woolum, Janet, *Outstanding Women Athletes: Who They Are and How They Influenced Sports in America.* Phoenix, Arizona: Oryx Press, 1992, p. 30.

1979 ▪ **Ann Meyers** was the first woman to sign a contract to play in the National Basketball Association. On August 30, 1979, she signed a one-year contract with the Indiana Pacers.

Source: Woolum, Janet, *Outstanding Women Athletes: Who They Are and How They Influenced Sports in America.* Phoenix, Arizona: Oryx Press, 1992, p. 30.

Lynette Woodard was the first female player on the Harlem Globetrotters basketball team.

1981 ▪ **Betty Ellis** (1941-), an American athletic official, became the first woman to officiate at a professional soccer game. Hired by the North American Soccer League as a referee, she officiated a match between the San José Earthquakes and the Edmonton Drillers on May 10, 1981.

Source: Read, Phyllis J., and Bernard L. Witlieb, *The Book of Women's Firsts.* New York: Random House, 1992, p. 144.

1982 ▪ The first women's basketball championship sponsored by the National Collegiate Athletic Association (NCAA) took place on March 28, 1982. Louisiana Tech defeated Cheney State 76-62.

Source: Woolum, Janet, *Outstanding Women Athletes: Who They Are and How They Influenced Sports in America.* Phoenix, Arizona: Oryx Press, 1992, p. 30.

1985 ▪ **Lynette Woodard** (1959-), an American basketball player, became the first female player for the Harlem Globetrotters (an all-male basketball team that blended entertaining highjinks with serious play). Woodard played in her first Globetrotters' game in Seattle, Washington, on November 13, 1985. A four-time collegiate All-American, Woodard set several records during her career. She played on the U.S. Olympic basketball team in 1984, winning a gold medal. In 1981 she received the Wade Trophy and the Broderick Award as the outstanding U.S. collegiate basketball player. In more recent years, Woodard was a driving force in the formation of the Women's National Basketball Association (WNBA).

Source: Read, Phyllis J., and Bernard L. Witlieb, *The Book of Women's Firsts.* New York: Random House, 1992, p. 493.

1986 ▪ **Nancy Lieberman** (1958-), an American basketball player, became the first woman to play on a men's professional basketball team when she played for the Springfield Fame, a Massachusetts team of the United States Basketball League. (The team's name reflected the fact that Springfield is home to the Basketball Hall of Fame.) The ball from this historic game was placed in the Boston Museum of Science. A three-time All-American basketball player at Old Dominion University from 1978 to 1980, Lieberman went on to a career as a sportscaster for ESPN and Prime Network. She covered the Continental Basketball Association women's basketball games.

Source: Read, Phyllis J., and Bernard L. Witlieb, *The Book of Women's Firsts.* New York: Random House, 1992, pp. 252-53.

1988 ▪ **Julie Croteau,** an American baseball player, was the first woman to play on a men's collegiate baseball team. She took the field for National Collegiate Athletic Association (NCAA) Division III St. Mary's College of Maryland in 1988.

Source: Woolum, Janet, *Outstanding Women Athletes: Who They Are and How They Influenced Sports in America.* Phoenix, Arizona: Oryx Press, 1992, p. 30.

1990 ▪ **Bernadette Locke,** an American basketball coach, became the first woman to coach a major college men's sport when she accepted the position of assistant coach on the University of Kentucky men's basketball team in June 1990.

Source: Woolum, Janet, *Outstanding Women Athletes: Who They Are and How They Influenced Sports in America.* Phoenix, Arizona: Oryx Press, 1992, p. 31.

1991 ▪ Barbara Hedges, an American educator, was named athletic director for the University of Washington in May 1991. Hedges was the first female athletic director of a National Collegiate Athletic Association (NCAA) Division I school that included football.

Source: Woolum, Janet, *Outstanding Women Athletes: Who They Are and How They Influenced Sports in America.* Phoenix, Arizona: Oryx Press, 1992, p. 31.

1991 ▪ Judy Sweet, an American educator, became the first female president of the National Collegiate Athletic Association (NCAA).

Source: Woolum, Janet, *Outstanding Women Athletes: Who They Are and How They Influenced Sports in America.* Phoenix, Arizona: Oryx Press, 1992, p. 31.

1991 ▪ Sandra Ortiz-Del Valle (1951-), an American basketball official, was the first woman to officiate a men's professional basketball game. She refereed the United States Basketball League (USBL) game between the New Haven Skyhawks and the Philadelphia Spirit on July 15, 1991.

Source: Woolum, Janet, *Outstanding Women Athletes: Who They Are and How They Influenced Sports in America.* Phoenix, Arizona: Oryx Press, 1992, p. 31.

1991 ▪ The United States soccer team won the first Women's World Soccer Championship. The U.S. team defeated Norway in final playoffs on November 30, 1991, in Guangzhov, China.

Source: Read, Phyllis J., and Bernard L. Witlieb, *The Book of Women's Firsts.* New York: Random House, 1992, p. 413.

1992 ▪ Manon Rheaume, a Canadian hockey player, became the first woman to play in the National Hockey League (NHL). A hockey goaltender since the age of five, Rheaume was the first girl to play in Canada's Major Junior Hockey League. She joined the Tampa Bay (Florida) Lightning and played her first exhibition game in the NHL in October 1992.

Source: *Time,* October 5, 1992.

1994 ▪ **Ila Borders,** an American athlete, was the first woman to pitch for a men's collegiate baseball team. Playing for Southern California College, she pitched against Claremont Mudd-Scripps in Cosa Mesa, California, on February 22, 1994. Southern California defeated Claremont Mudd-Scripps 12-1. Borders hopes to become a major league baseball pitcher.

Source: *The New York Times,* February 23, 1994.

1995 ▪ The first all-women's crew entered the America's Cup race. The initial 22 crew members, selected from 650 applicants, included five Olympic medalists and six experienced yacht racers. Among them were: J. J. Isler, two-time Rolex Yachtswoman of the Year and the first woman captain of the sailing team at Yale University; Shelly Beattie, better known as Siren on the television program *American Gladiators;* and Susie Nairn, an aerospace engineer in the microgravity division at the National Aeronautics and Space Administration (NASA). The crew was sponsored by yacht racer and financier Bill Koch.

Source: *People Weekly.* February 20, 1995, p. 84.

1995 ▪ **Sheryl Swoopes,** an American basketball player, was the first woman to have an athletic shoe named after her. The sportswear company Nike named the woman's basketball shoe "Air Swoopes," honoring the former all-American from Texas Tech University and Olympic gold medalist. In August 1997, three weeks after giving birth to her son Eric, Swoopes began her professional basketball career with the Houston Comets of the Women's National Basketball Association.

Source: Drape, Joe, "Bouncing Ball, Bouncing Baby Boy," *The New York Times.* August 3, 1997.

Travel and Adventure

1871 ▪ **Lucy Walker** (1836-1916), an English mountaineer, was the first woman to climb the Matterhorn, in Switzerland. Walker reached the summit (mountain top) on July 20, 1871. She was also the first woman to climb two other Swiss peaks, the Weisshorn and the Lyskamm. Walker was one of the first members of the Ladies' Alpine Club (the first society for female mountaineers, founded in London in 1907) and served as the group's second president, beginning in 1912.

Source: Uglow, Jennifer S., ed., *The Continuum Dictionary of Women's Biography.* New York: Continuum, 1989, p. 565.

1877 ▪ **Anne King Blunt** (1837-1917) was the first English woman to travel in and describe the Arabian peninsula. Blunt left England for Turkey, Algiers, and Egypt in 1877, and in 1878 published her book, *The Bedouin Tribes of the Euphrates.*

Source: Uglow, Jennifer S., ed., *The Continuum Dictionary of Women's Biography.* New York: Continuum, 1989, p. 73.

1888 ▪ **Katy Richardson** (1864-1927), an English mountaineer, was the first person to climb the Aiguille de Bionnassay and to travel the eastern ridge of the Dome de Gouter—a route previously thought impossible—in the French Alps. Richardson's remarkable athletic career between 1882 and 1893 included six pioneer first ascents and 14 first ascents by a woman.

Source: Uglow, Jennifer S., ed., *The Continuum Dictionary of Women's Biography.* New York: Continuum, 1989, p. 457.

Newpaperwoman Nellie Bly beat the 80-day around-the-world record set by fictional Phineas Fogg in Jules Verne's Around the World in Eighty Days.

1890 ▪ **Nellie Bly** (pseudonym of Elizabeth Cochrane Seaman; 1865-1922), an American journalist, was the first woman to beat the 80-day around-the-world record set by the fictional Phineas Fogg in Jules Verne's *Around the World in Eighty Days.* Bly's New York City newspaper, *The World,* sent her on the mission, which she accomplished traveling by train, handcar, ship, and burro. Bly sailed from Hoboken, New Jersey, on November 14, 1889, and arrived 72 days later by train in New York City on January 25, 1890.

Woman Biked Around the World

Annie Loudonberry, an American cyclist, was the first woman to make a bicycle trip around the world. She began her journey on June 26, 1894, at the State House in Boston, Massachusetts, and finished on September 12, 1895 in Chicago, Illinois. Loudonberry collected a $10,000 bet for completing the trip within 15 months.

Source: Read, Phyllis J., and Bernard L. Witlieb, *The Book of Women's Firsts.* New York: Random House, 1992, pp. 57-58.

1890 ▪ **Fay Fuller,** an American mountain climber, was the first woman to reach the summit of Mount Rainier in Washington state. With a blanket roll and a walking stick as her only equipment, Fuller reached the summit (mountain top) on August 10, 1890.

Source: McCullough, Joan, *First of All: Significant "Firsts" by American Women.* New York: Holt, 1980, p. 149.

1892 ▪ Isabella Bird Bishop (1831-1904), a British traveler, was the first woman elected a member of the Royal Geographical Society in England. One of the first female world explorers, she wrote travelogues about her experiences in Asia.

Source: Parry, Melanie, ed., *Larousse Dictionary of Women.* New York: Larousse Kingfisher Chambers, Inc., 1995, p. 179.

1901 ▪ **Anna Edson Taylor** (1858-1921), an American adventurer, was the first woman to succeed in going over Niagara Falls. On October 24, 1901, riding in a barrel, Taylor went over Horseshoe Falls, on the Canadian side of Niagara Falls. She completed this feat for a cash award, which she used to pay off a loan on a ranch in Texas.

Source: Read, Phyllis J., and Bernard L. Witlieb, *The Book of Women's Firsts.* New York: Random House, 1992, p. 438.

1907 ▪ **Elizabeth Le Blond** (1861-1934), a British mountain climber, was the first president of the Ladies' Alpine Club in London, England. This club, the female counterpart of the all-male Alpine Club, encouraged mountaineering and scientific discovery. Le Blond achieved a number of climbing firsts. In the 1890s she was the first woman to lead climbing parties without local guides and, in 1900, accompanied by her friend Lady Evelyn McDonnel, Le Blond was the first woman to climb with ropes during an ascent of Italian peak Piz Palu.

Source: Uglow, Jennifer S., ed., *The Continuum Dictionary of Women's Biography.* New York: Continuum, 1989, p. 317.

1908 ▪ Annie Smith Peck (1850-1935), an American mountaineer, was the first person to climb the north peak of Mount Huascaran in Peru. With an altitude of 21,812 feet, this was—at the time—the highest altitude reached by any climber in the Western Hemisphere.

Source: James, Edward T., and others, eds., *Notable American Women, 1607-1950: A Biographical Dictionary.* Cambridge, Massachusetts: Harvard University Press, 1971, pp. 40-42.

1913 ▪ Georgia "Tiny" Broadwick (1895-1978), an American parachutist, was the first woman to free-fall parachute from an airplane. On June 21, 1913, Broadwick jumped from a plane flying at 1,000 feet near Los Angeles, California, and landed safely in a barley field.

Source: Read, Phyllis J., and Bernard L. Witlieb, *The Book of Women's Firsts.* New York: Random House, 1992, p. 69.

1916 ▪ Adeline and Augusta Van Buren, sisters from New York, were the first women to cross the continental United States on motorcycles. The purpose of the sisters' trip was to convince the U.S. government that women were capable of serving in the armed forces should the United States enter World War I (1914-1918). When Adeline Van Buren volunteered for the army in 1917, however, she was rejected because of her sex.

Source: Read, Phyllis J., and Bernard L. Witlieb, *The Book of Women's Firsts.* New York: Random House, 1992, pp. 460-61.

1921 ▪ Bessie Coleman (1893-1926), an American aviator, was the first African-American female pilot; she was also the first woman from the United States to earn an international pilot's license. Coleman gave stunt shows worldwide and died while rehearsing for an exhibition for the Jacksonville, Florida, Negro Welfare League.

Source: Smith, Jessie Carney, *Black Firsts: 2000 Years of Extraordinary Achievement.* Detroit: Gale Research Inc., 1994, p. 255.

1924 ▪ **Alexandra David-Neel** (1869-1968), a French explorer of Central Asia, was the first European woman to enter the holy city of Lhasa in Tibet. She entered the city disguised as an old Tibetan woman. David-Neel went on to write several books about her experiences, including *My Journey to Lhasa* (1927).

Source: Magnusson, Magnus, *Larousse Biographical Dictionary.* Edinburgh: Larousse Kingfisher Chambers, Inc., 1994, p. 389.

1928 ▪ **Sophia Heath** (1890-1934), an English aviator, became the first woman to fly solo from South Africa to England. She soon after became the first person to land at 50 different airfields and 17 unofficial landing fields, achieving a record of 67 landings in England in a single day. She was also the first airline pilot for the Royal Dutch Airlines in the 1920s. An advocate of women's athletics, Heath founded the Women's Amateur Athletic Association, in England in 1922. As a result of her work on behalf of women in sports, women competed in track and field medal events at the Olympics for the first time in 1928.

Source: Chicago, Judy, *The Dinner Party.* New York: Anchor, 1979, p. 193.

1930 ▪ **Amy Johnson** (later, Johnson-Mollison; 1903-1941), an English aviator, was the first woman to fly solo from London to Australia. She was also the first woman to pass the test for the British Ground Engineers' License and the first woman to fly across the Atlantic Ocean from east to west. Johnson and her husband, James Allen Mollison, took off from Pendine, Wales, on July 22, 1933, and crash-landed 38 hours later at Stratford, Connecticut. Johnson died while flying for the Women's Auxiliary Air Force (WAAFs) during World War II (1939-1945).

Source: Kane, Nathan Joseph, *Famous First Facts.* New York: H. W. Wilson, 1981, p. 87.

1930 ▪ **Laura Ingalls,** an American aviator, was the first woman to complete a transcontinental flight. She left Roosevelt

Field, New York, in a Moth bi-plane on October 5, 1930, and landed in Glendale, California, on October 9. The trip required nine stops and took 30 hours and 27 minutes.

Source: Read, Phyllis J., and Bernard L. Witlieb, *The Book of Women's Firsts.* New York: Random House, 1992, pp. 225-26.

1932 ▪ Miriam Underhill (1900-), an American mountaineer, was the first woman to lead a group composed of women on a successful ascent of the Matterhorn in Switzerland. The women reached the summit on August 12, 1932. Underhill was also the first woman to pioneer a route to the Torre Grande in the Italian Dolomites, a route now called the "Via Miriam," in 1927. The following year Underhill made the first traverse of the Grépon led by a woman, and she became the first person to complete a traverse of the Aiguille du Diable, both in the Alps.

Source: Uglow, Jennifer S., ed., *The Continuum Dictionary of Women's Biography.* New York: Continuum, 1989, p. 552.

1934 ▪ Anne Spencer Morrow Lindbergh (b. 1906), an American pilot, was the first woman to receive the National Geographic Society Hubbard Gold Medal. Anne Lindbergh was honored for her work as copilot and radio operator on flights with her husband, famous aviator Charles A. Lindbergh (1902-1974). The couple flew over five continents to survey transoceanic air routes, and the results of their work became known as the *Charles A. Lindbergh Aerial Survey.* Anne Lindbergh was presented the medal on March 31, 1934, by the president of the National Geographic Society.

Source: Kane, Nathan Joseph, *Famous First Facts.* New York: H. W. Wilson, 1981, p. 373.

1948 ▪ Jacqueline Cochran (1910-1980), the first female jet pilot, became the first woman to achieve Mach 1 (the speed of sound), on May 18, 1948. She achieved this record in an F-86

Amelia Earhart

Amelia Earhart achieved many firsts as an pilot. In 1932 she was the first woman to complete a solo transatlantic (overseas) flight. A few years later, in 1935, Earhart completed the first solo flight from California to Hawaii. Attempting a flight around the world in 1937, Earhart lost contact with the Coast Guard near Howland Island in the Pacific, where she is presumed to have died when her plane went into the ocean.

Pilot Jacqueline Cochran
was the first woman to
achieve Mach 1 (the
speed of sound).

jet. Cochran started flying in 1932 and was the first woman to enter the Trans-American Bendix Race. She was the first living woman inducted into the American Aviation Hall of Fame in 1971.

Source: Parry, Melanie, ed., *Larousse Dictionary of Women*. New York: Larousse Kingfisher Chambers, Inc., 1995, p. 153.

1954 ▪ **Claude Kogan** (1919-1959), a French mountaineer, had a distinguished career that included a number of firsts. In 1954 she was the first European woman to climb Cho Oyo, a peak in the Himalayas, reaching a height of 25,000 feet, the highest point ever reached by a European woman. Earlier, Kogan was the first woman to reach the top of Sakantay in Peru's Cordillera Vilcabamba and the first person to climb Nun in the Punjab. In 1955 she was the first person to ascend Ganesh Himal in the Himalayan range. Kogan was also the first person to address a joint meeting of the Ladies' Alpine Club and the Alpine Club, in London in the mid-1950s. She died while leading an all-female party on an ascent of Cho Oyo.

Source: Uglow, Jennifer S., ed., *The Continuum Dictionary of Women's Biography.* New York: Continuum, 1989, p. 302.

1955 ▪ The "Whirly Girls" were the first American association of female helicopter pilots. At the time the group formed, there were only 13 licensed female helicopter pilots in the world.

Source: Read, Phyllis J., and Bernard L. Witlieb, *The Book of Women's Firsts.* New York: Random House, 1992, p. 478.

1956 ▪ **Maria Atanassova,** a Russian pilot, was the first female pilot to work for a commercial airline. She was made a full pilot for the Soviet airline Aeroflot in 1956. Atanassova caused a sensation when she landed at Heathrow Airport in England in 1966, because it was the first time a woman had piloted a large jet aircraft at an airport outside of Russia.

Source: Sanders, Dennis, *The First of Everything.* New York: Delacorte Press, 1981, p. 100.

1964 ▪ **Donna Mae Mins,** an American sports car driver, became the first woman to win a Sports Car Club of America championship. She beat out 31 men in the Class II production category for imported two-seat sports cars.

Source: Woolum, Janet, *Outstanding Women Athletes: Who They Are and How They Influenced Sports in America.* Phoenix, Arizona: Oryx Press, 1992, p. 28.

1964 ▪ **Geraldine (Jerrie) Mock** (1925-) became the first woman to fly solo around the world when she completed her flight in a single-engine plane. She took off from Port Columbus, Ohio, on March 19, 1964, made 21 stops, and logged 22,858.8 miles before returning home on April 17.

Source: Read, Phyllis J., ed., and Bernard L. Witlieb, *The Book of Women's Firsts.* New York: Random House, 1992, pp. 295-96.

1965 ▪ **Margaret Laneive "Lee" Breedlove** set a women's land speed record at 308.65 miles per hour on the Bonneville Salt Flats, Utah, on November 4, 1965.

Source: Woolum, Janet, *Outstanding Women Athletes: Who They Are and How They Influenced Sports in America.* Phoenix, Arizona: Oryx Press, 1992, p. 28.

1966 ▪ **Anne Burns,** an English flyer, was the first woman to win the British Glider Championships, held in England in 1966. She had an international reputation in this sport and had twice been honored with the Queen's Commendation for valuable service in the air, in 1955 and 1963.

Source: O'Neill, Lois Decker, ed., *The Women's Book of World Records and Achievements.* Garden City, New York: Doubleday, 1979, p. 591.

1969 ▪ **Sharon Sites Adams** (1930-), an American sailor, became the first woman to sail a boat alone across the Pacific Ocean. Adams left Yokohama, Japan, on May 12 and arrived in San Diego, California, on July 25, covering approximately 5,620 miles in 74 days, 17 hours, and 15 minutes.

Source: Read, Phyllis J., and Bernard L. Witlieb, *The Book of Women's Firsts.* New York: Random House, 1992, p. 8.

1969 ▪ **Audrey McElmury,** an American cyclist, won the women's world road racing championship in Bruno, Czechoslovakia. With her victory, McElmury became the first American—man or woman—to win a world road racing title.

Source: Woolum, Janet, *Outstanding Women Athletes: Who They Are and How They Influenced Sports in America.* Phoenix, Arizona: Oryx Press, 1992, p. 28.

1971 ▪ **Sheila Christine Scott** (1927-1988), an English aviator, was the first person to make a solo light aircraft flight around the world. She flew equator to equator over the North

Pole in 1971. Scott was also the founder and first governor of the British section of the Ninety-nines and founder of the British Balloon and Airships Club. (The Ninety-nines was the first organization for licensed women pilots. Founded in 1929, the club was so named because 99 out of the 126 pilots joined.)

Source: Uglow, Jennifer S., ed., *The Continuum Dictionary of Women's Biography.* New York: Continuum, 1989, p. 489.

1975 ▪ Karren Stead (1964-) became the first girl to win the National Soap Box Derby on August 3, 1975, in Akron, Ohio. In addition to the title, Stead won a $3,000 scholarship.

Source: McCullough, Joan, *First of All: Significant "Firsts" by American Women.* New York: Holt, 1980, p. 154.

1975 ▪ Junko Tabei (1939-), a Japanese mountaineer, was the first woman to reach the summit of Mount Everest. As deputy leader of an all-female Japanese expedition, Tabei reached the top on May 16, 1975.

Source: *The (Cleveland) Plain Dealer.* May 19, 1996.

In May of 1976 Janet Guthrie was the first woman to drive in the Indianapolis 500 auto race.

1975 ▪ Shirley Muldowney (1942-) became the first woman licensed in the United States to drive top fuel dragsters in 1975. Muldowney, known in drag racing as "Cha Cha," was also the first woman to qualify for the top competition in hot rod racing when she qualified to compete in the supercharged, nitro-burning, unlimited AA-fuel dragster category.

Source: O'Neill, Lois Decker, ed., *The Women's Book of World Records and Achievements.* Garden City, New York: Doubleday, 1979, p. 589.

1976 ▪ Janet Guthrie (1938-), an American race car driver, became the first woman to compete in a major stock car race. (A stock car is a race car that has the chassis of a commercially produced, assembly-line model.) She competed in the World

Shirley Muldowney was the first woman licensed in the United States to drive top fuel dragsters.

600 in Charlotte, North Carolina, on May 30, 1976. She finished in fifteenth place among 40 drivers, winning $3,555. Guthrie became the first woman to drive in the Indianapolis 500 auto race when she qualified to enter in May of 1976. She failed to finish the race because her car broke down, but on May 29, 1978, she tried again and became the first woman to complete this race, finishing eighth among the 33 other drivers.

Source: Read, Phyllis J., and Bernard L. Witlieb, *The Book of Women's Firsts.* New York: Random House, 1992, pp. 187-88.

1976 ▪ **Mary McGee,** an American driver of cars, trucks, and motorcycles, was the first woman to race in the Baja 1000 off-road competition in California. She was also the first woman to compete in the Mexico Wild Desert Peninsula Race, the first to race in the International Motocross Series, and the first to drive in Grand Prix motorcycle tournaments.

Source: O'Neill, Lois Decker, ed., *The Women's Book of World Records and Achievements.* Garden City, New York: Doubleday, 1979, p. 590.

1977 ▪ **Clare Mary Francis** (1946-), an English sailor, was the first female skipper (head of the crew) in the Whitbread Round the World Event. Francis and her crew placed fifth in the 1977-1978 Whitbread competition. In 1976 Francis was the first and only woman to finish the Royal Western Singlehanded Transatlantic Race, from Falmouth, England, to Newport, Rhode Island. She has written both nonfictional and fictional books based on her experiences as a woman at sea,

Source: Uglow, Jennifer S., ed., *The Continuum Dictionary of Women's Biography.* New York: Continuum, 1989, p. 211.

Riddles Won Iditarod

Libby Riddles (1956-), an American dogsled driver, became the first woman to win the Iditarod Trail Sled Dog Race on March 20, 1985. The annual race is a 1,100-mile (1,827-kilometer) marathon from Anchorage to Nome, Alaska.

1977 ▪ At age 50, **Betty Cook** (1927-), an American motorboat racer, became the first woman to win a major offshore motorboat race. She placed first in the Bushmills Grand Prix off Newport Beach, California, on March 27, 1977.

Source: Woolum, Janet, *Outstanding Women Athletes: Who They Are and How They Influenced Sports in America.* Phoenix, Arizona: Oryx Press, 1992, p. 29.

1977 ▪ **Marie Ledbetter** was the first woman to win the World Accuracy Title in parachuting. She achieved this record at the twelfth annual Parachuting Championship in Rome, Italy, in 1977. In eight jumps from 2,500 feet, her total accumulated distance from the target was less than four feet.

Source: O'Neill, Lois Decker, ed., *The Women's Book of World Records and Achievements.* Garden City, New York: Doubleday, 1979, p. 591.

1978 ▪ **Arlene Blum,** led the first all-female expedition to climb Annapurna, the world's tenth-highest mountain, in the Himalayan mountains in Nepal. The team succeeded in reaching the summit in 1978. Two women died in the attempt.

Source: Read, Phyllis J., and Bernard L. Witlieb, *The Book of Women's Firsts.* New York: Random House, 1992, p. 206.

1986 ▪ **Ann Bancroft** (1955-) was the first woman to walk to the North Pole when she and her five male companions reached the North Pole by dogsled on May 1, 1986. A physical education teacher, Bancroft endured 12-hour days and numerous hardships as she and her team and 21 dogs completed the expedition.

Source: Read, Phyllis J., and Bernard L. Witlieb, *The Book of Women's Firsts.* New York: Random House, 1992, p. 35.

1986 ▪ **Jeana Yeager** (1952-) was the first woman to fly nonstop around the world without refueling. She began her trip at Edwards Air Force Base in the Mojave Desert of California on December 14, 1986, and returned on December 23. With copilot Dick Rutan, Yeager flew a lightweight craft, called the *Voyager,* designed by Dick's brother Burt.

Source: Read, Phyllis J., and Bernard L. Witlieb, *The Book of Women's Firsts.* New York: Random House, 1992, p. 499.

1990 ▪ **Susan Butcher,** an American sled dog racer, set the Iditarod speed record. (The Iditarod is an annual 1,100-mile [1,827-kilometer] dogsled marathon from Anchorage to Nome, Alaska.) Butcher won the race four times, in 1986, 1987, 1988, and 1990. The National Academy of Sports named her Outstanding Female Athlete in 1989.

Source: Parry, Melanie, ed., *Larousse Dictionary of Women.* New York: Larousse Kingfisher Chambers, Inc., 1995, p. 112.

1991 ▪ **Vojai Reed** became the first woman to compete in a Bass Anglers Sportsman Society tournament in 1991. The Missouri Invitational at Truman Lake was run by the U.S. Army Corps of Engineers, who threatened to cancel the tournament if women were not allowed to participate.

Source: *Sports Illustrated.* May 13, 1991.

Index

Bold type indicates main entries
Italic type indicates volume numbers
Illustrations are marked by (ill.)

*Rita Dove (see "The Arts:
Literature" entry dated
1993)*

411